BARACK 'EM UP

A LITERARY INVESTIGATION

By

Lloyd Billingsley

A Centershot Book

Copyright © 2017 by Lloyd Billingsley

All rights reserved.

No part of this book may be reproduced or transmitted in any form or by any means, electronic or mechanical, including photocopying, recording or by any information storage and retrieval system, without written permission from the author, except for the inclusion of brief quotations in review.

Also by Lloyd Billingsley

Bill of Writes: Dispatches from the Political Correctness Battlefield

Hollywood Party: Stalinist Adventures in the American Movie Industry

Shotgun Weddings: The Saga of Grandma Cokey, California's Serial Husband Killer

Exceptional Depravity: Dan Who Likes Dark and Double Murder in Davis, California

ISBN 978-0-9968581-2-0 (pbk.)

First edition 2016

Printed in the United States of America

1 2 3 4 5 6 7 8 9 10

For RG

A harmful truth is better than a useful lie.
— Thomas Mann

The persons and events in this book are factual. Any resemblance to fictitious persons or imaginary events is entirely coincidental.

Table of Contents

"Half-Kenyan." 3
"A stubborn desire to protect myself from scrutiny." 6
"Barry, is this you?" 11
"Barack is such a beautiful name." 19
"They'll drive you to drink, boy." 28
"Respect came from what you did and not who your daddy was." ...35
"The Old Man used to talk about you so much!" 43
"A black man from Kansas named Frank." 54
"I am a prisoner of my own biography." 60
"We are five days away." 68
"My heart is filled with love for this country." 79
"Quite a few coeds are available for special affairs." 90
"A kind of truth." 99
"Obama said nothing of his new girlfriend." 107
"Remarkable similarities." 111
"His dad taught him to love jazz." 115
"Biography is foundational." 120
"The narrative skill of a gifted novelist." 125
"Axelfraud." 133
"Without any question a work of historical fiction." 138

"Half-Kenyan."

On Monday, July 25, 2016, at the Democratic National Convention in Philadelphia, First Lady Michelle Obama stepped up to the podium.

"Don't let anyone ever tell you that this country is not great, that somehow we need to make it great again," the First Lady, elegantly clad in blue, told the cheering crowd. "Because this right now is the greatest country on Earth."

Early in her speech, by some accounts the best of the convention, the First Lady spoke of the challenges she and her husband face as they guide daughters Malia and Natasha in the spotlight of public life.

"We urge them to ignore those who question their father's citizenship or faith," the First Lady said.

For Michelle Obama, such questions remained an issue even though her husband had been President of the United States, the most powerful man in the world, for nearly eight years, and lately had been surging in popularity. On Wednesday, July 27, poised and eloquent as always, the president himself would address the convention.

Proclaiming himself "more optimistic than ever before," President Obama told the crowd he had made "health care a right for everybody" and "brought troops home." His administration had "delivered justice to Osama Bin Laden" and through diplomacy, the president said, "we shut down Iran's nuclear weapons program," but it wasn't only about his triumphs.

The two-term president was ready to pass the baton to former First Lady and Secretary of State Hillary Clinton, a person in his view more qualified than anyone to be president and "fit and ready to be commander-in-chief." That had eager conventioneers chanting "four more years!" but it wasn't all about passing the torch.

During the course of his speech, by some accounts his best ever, the president duly invoked his Kansas grandparents. "Their ancestors began settling there about 200 years ago," he said. "I don't know if they had their birth certificates, but they were there." The president also told the convention about his grandparents' "half-Kenyan grandson," a reference to the story he brokered at the Democratic convention in 2004:

"My father was a foreign student, born and raised in a small village in Kenya. He grew up herding goats, went to school in a tin-roof shack. His father, my grandfather, was a cook, a domestic servant to the British."

For the Democratic Party faithful and media establishment, that story had long been a matter of record, but shortly before the president's 2016 convention speech some doubts had surfaced.

"Words of Obama's Father Still Waiting to be Read by His Son," headlined a June 18, 2016, *New York Times* story by Rachel L. Swarns, about a cache of documents from the Kenyan Barack H. Obama dating from 1958 to 1964. An archivist with the Harlem-based Schomburg Center for Research in Black Culture made the discovery in 2013 and invited the President of the United States to come and have a look. The president declined the invitation and by Father's Day, 2016, he still had not reviewed the material. The lapse left some observers puzzled, but the president had good reason for his inaction. In not a single document, including more than 20 letters, did the Kenyan Barack H. Obama mention anything about his new American wife and Hawaiian-born American son.

Back in 2008, some had questioned whether the candidate Barack Obama was born in the United States, but this was something of a moot point. Even if he had been born abroad, his American mother, Ann Dunham, made him an American citizen fully eligible for office. Even so, the handsome, eloquent candidate was not exactly forthcoming with documentation on key aspects of his life.

If there was anything truly amiss in the candidate's background, some observers thought at the time, Hillary Clinton, a former First Lady with powerful friends in the media and intelligence community, would have dug it up in the primaries and deployed it to smack down her opponent. She did not do so, and that year the candidate Barack Obama became President of the United States. Even so, the most powerful man in the world could not make the mysteries about his background disappear, and during the president's second term they mounted a surge.

In 2012, *The Communist*, by Grove City College political science professor Paul Kengor, made a strong case that the president's ideological mentor was not a Kenyan foreign student of humble origins. He was Frank Marshall Davis, an African-American Stalinist of unusual ferocity, and with an FBI file some 600 pages long. The old-line establishment media for the most part ignored the book, subtitled *Frank Marshall Davis: the Untold Story of Barack Obama's Mentor*. In 2015, the *Washington Post* gave three Pinocchios to *The Communist*, one less than the *Post* gave the president for his claim that if you liked your health plan you could keep it, which the *New York Times* called an "incorrect promise."

Dreams from My Real Father, a 2012 documentary film by Joel Gilbert, contended that Davis, a faithful pro-Soviet Communist who made a name for himself in Chicago, was the president's biological father. In 2015, Mr. Gilbert tracked down Malik Obama, son of the Kenyan Barack Obama, who noted a strong resemblance between the president and Frank Marshall Davis, right down to the spots on their faces.

"I don't know how I'd deal with it, if it really came out that he really is a fraud or a con," Malik Obama told Gilbert. The Kenyan even offered to take a DNA test, but that drew no response from the president's handlers. As far as Mr. Gilbert knows, nobody in the media has ever asked the president about his relationship to Frank Marshall Davis.

After the revelations of *The Communist* and *Dreams from My Real Father*, some observers expected an insider to step forward and tell all. Nobody volunteered, but that had already been done. In the Dead Sea Scrolls of the president's story, the ultimate insiders left the keys near the front door.

"A stubborn desire to protect myself from scrutiny."

Dreams from My Father appeared in 1995 in a hardcover edition from Times Books that is now a collector's item, with signed copies selling on the Internet for thousands of dollars. The name on the cover was Barack Obama, a relative unknown with no other books to his credit and little, if any, record of publication. He had written no news stories, no reviews or features, and no thoughtful essays that anybody could find.

The cover shows a photo of an African woman with a male child seated on her lap. No man appears in the picture. The 2004 edition bears a photo of the American Barack Obama looking to his right at the photo of the African woman and her male child. On Obama's left, the cover shows a photo of a middle-aged white male in a military uniform and a female child. The man in the middle, observers might assume, somehow proceeds from the African boy and American girl in the photos. The book contains no photos other than the three on the cover.

Dreams from My Father does not indicate who took the photo of the African woman and her male child, what year it was taken, and does not identify the African woman and child in the picture. Apparently readers are to judge the book by its cover and assume the photo shows Barack Obama's father and his paternal grandmother. That is a central theme of the book, which bears a curious biblical epigraph from 1 Chronicles 29:15:

"For we are strangers before them, and sojourners, as were all our fathers."

So this book will be dealing with "strangers," as all our fathers were. Actually, for most readers, their fathers weren't strangers at all, even though that's what the Bible says. Other identity questions emerge in the foreword, as on page ix.

"I confess to wincing every so often at a poorly chosen word, a mangled sentence, an expression of emotion that seems indulgent or overly practiced. I have the urge to cut the book by fifty pages or so," says the author. "I cannot honestly say, however, that the voice in this book is not mine."

The sentence recalls Eric Idle's tribute to the film director who "has only done more than not anyone." The author's poorly chosen mangled sentence stayed in, with good reason. As George Orwell noted in his famous essay, "Politics and the English Language," the great enemy of clear language is insincerity.

"I can honestly say that the voice in this book is mine," would be much cleaner, but why say even that if there was no question about the voice in the book? Those who write their own books never raise questions about the "voice" in their work. The man named on the cover of *Dreams from My Father* explains that he got help – from his mother.

"We saw each other frequently, our bonds unbroken," he says. "During the writing of this book, she would read the drafts, correcting stories that I had misunderstood, careful not to comment on my characterizations of her but quick to explain or defend the less flattering aspects of my father's character."

Note that any question about the voice in the book is due to the mother's editorial role, and that centered not on herself but the author's father. This man, not named here, has some kind of character problem, though readers do not learn what the "less flattering" aspects of his character might be, and what his mother said about them. The reader can't go to the primary source because the author's mother, Ann Dunham, passed away in November, 1995, but down the road it became evident that not much correcting, if any, ever took place.

In the introduction, the author explains, "we have all seen too much to take my parents' brief union – a black man and white woman, an African and an American, at face value." As a result, "people have a hard time taking me at face value."

The author, in effect, telegraphs it with a flare gun, and he's just getting started.

"Well," he writes, "I suspect that I sound incurably naïve, wedded to lost hopes, like those Communists who peddle their newspapers on the fringes of various college towns."

So on page xv of the introduction, before the main text even starts, the author introduces the word "Communists," upper case his. This is not a term most readers would expect to find. *Dreams from My Father* purports to be a story about a black American and his elusive Kenyan father. Communism was the ideology of white Europeans, and the context is also important.

During the time of writing, the early 1990s, after the demise of the Soviet Union and the fall of the Berlin Wall, Communists were sulking in the loser's locker room. Given its pretensions to create a better world for all, Communism is a strong contender for the greatest failure in history. Communist regimes were big on utopian rhetoric but barren of liberties and barren of groceries. In the USSR, as Ronald Kessler detailed in *Moscow Station*, people had to wait in three lines to buy consumer goods: one line to select the item, one line to pay for it, and a third line to pick it up.

The Communists' greatest success was the murder of countless millions and if readers have any doubt, they can refer to carefully documented works such as *The Great Terror*, *Harvest of Sorrow*, *The Black Book of Communism*, *Bloodlands: Europe Between Hitler and Stalin*, and many others. As Albert Camus put it, Communism equals murder.

The author of *Dreams from My Father* shows no kinship whatsoever with the millions liberated from the Communist regimes. At the time this book was written they were celebrating their newfound freedom but the author does not celebrate with them. Poland's brave Solidarity activists, facing down martial law imposed by a Soviet puppet regime, get no ink here at all. On the other hand, this author is wedded to lost hopes he associates with Communists.

"Or worse," as he explains, "I sound like I'm trying to hide from myself."

He is taking evasive action and takes pains to explain it.

"I don't fault people their suspicions," the author says. "I learned long ago to distrust my childhood and the stories that shaped it. It was only many years later, after I had sat at my father's grave and spoken to him through Africa's red soil, that I could circle back and evaluate these early stories for myself. Or, more accurately, it was only then that I understood that I had spent much of my life trying to rewrite these stories, plugging up the holes in the narrative, accommodating unwelcome details, projecting individual choices against the blind sweep of history, all in the hope of extracting some granite slab of truth upon which my unborn children can stand."

Readers may want to spot-weld a few things here. The writer of this narrative has a deep need to conceal something about himself. As he admits, the people who have a hard time taking him at face value are justified in their suspicions. Indeed, the author himself has learned to distrust the stories that shaped his childhood. He had spent much of his life trying to "rewrite" those stories and acknowledges that some details are "unwelcome" but does not explain what the details are and why, exactly, they are unwelcome. And the writer concedes, he is up against "the blind sweep of history," but history is not blind – though some historians definitely are. Things happen, historical events like the Franco-Prussian War, Stalin's planned famine in Ukraine, and China's Cultural Revolution, but some people can choose to ignore the record.

"At some point then," the author says, "in spite of a stubborn desire to protect myself from scrutiny, in spite of the periodic impulse to abandon the entire project, what has found its way onto these pages is a record of a personal interior journey – a boy's search for his father, and through that search a workable meaning for his life as a black American."

This is a man with something to hide, so much so that he proclaims a "stubborn desire" to protect himself from scrutiny. One doubts the author got busted for indecent exposure, shoplifting or drunk driving, but what he has to hide must be rather serious because he considered dumping the whole book project before finally opting to proceed. Recall that he wanted to cut 50 pages, and that is a lot of material. Curious readers might check what presidential biographers, establishment journalists and other luminaries said about this openly acknowledged evasion.

At the time, readers in general and journalists in particular showed less interest in what the author had a stubborn desire to conceal than the story he wanted to tell. That one was about an "interior journey," and "a boy's search for his father."

The author with the stubborn to protect himself from scrutiny, and a father with a character problem, is no longer a boy in the fall of 1982, when he had just turned 21. As the narrative has it, (page 5) he was "in the middle of making myself breakfast, with coffee on the stove and two eggs on the skillet" when the phone rings and a roommate hands it to him. The line is thick with static.

"Barry, is this you?"

"Barry?" a voice says. "Barry, is this you?"
The voice is Aunt Jane in Nairobi. So the author's extended African family is simply assumed up front. They have been there all along, the reader is to understand, on a continent far away.

"Listen Barry, your father is dead," Aunt Jane from Nairobi says. "He is killed in a car accident. Hello? Can you hear me? I say, your father is dead. Barry, please call your uncle in Boston and tell him. I can't talk now, okay, Barry. I will try to call you again."

Aunt Jane does not name the uncle in Boston, nor explain why she didn't call him herself, or why she couldn't talk more now. And of course, "Barry" is not the same name readers see on the cover of *Dreams from My Father*.

"I sat down on the couch," the author says, "smelling eggs burn in the kitchen, staring at the cracks in the plaster, trying to measure my loss." The story continues:

"At the time of his death, my father remained a myth to me, both more and less than a man." Readers might wonder about the use of "myth," but the author explains. "He had left Hawaii back in 1963, when I was only two years old, so that as a child I knew him only through the stories that my mother and grandparents told."

As his mother explains, "Your father was a terrible driver. He'd end up on the left-hand side, the way the British drive, and if you said something, he'd just huff about silly American rules." And he was "puffing away on this pipe that I'd given him for his birthday party, pointing out all the sights with the stem, like a sea captain."

So the American son had partied it up with the Kenyan father, given him a pipe, and remembered the event in great detail. Grandma Toot, short for Tutu, meaning "grandparent" in Hawaiian, also contributes to the story. Later the author found other clues while rummaging through the closets.

"At the point where my own memories begin, my mother had already begun a courtship with a man who would become her second husband, and I sensed without explanation why the photographs had to be stored. But once in a while, the smell of dust and mothballs rising from the crumbling album, I would stare at my father's likeness – the dark laughing face, the prominent forehead and thick glasses that made him appear older than his years, and listen as the events of his life tumbled into a single narrative."

Instead of showing readers a photo, the author prefers a description. The myth, and all those stories that needed rewriting, have now become a single narrative as readers learn on page nine.

"He was an African, I would learn, a Kenyan of the Luo tribe, born on the shores of Lake Victoria in a place called Alego. . . my other grandfather, Hussein Onyango Obama, had been a prominent farmer, and elder of the tribe, a medicine man with healing powers. My father grew up herding his father's goats and attending the local school, set up by the British colonial administration, where he had shown great promise."

The African arrived at University of Hawaii in 1959 at age 23, the first African student there who "worked with unsurpassed concentration, and graduated in three years at top of his class." He also "helped organize the International Students Association, of which he became the first president."

The author does not explain how his father "became" president of the International Students Association. Was it by proclamation or was there an election? Who were the other candidates, and when did this take place? The author cites no documents or publications from the International Students Association, and no news stories about his father's presidency of the Association. On the other hand, the story has a romantic side.

"In a Russian language course, he met an awkward, shy American girl, only eighteen, and they fell in love. The girl's parents, wary at first, were won over by his charm and intellect; the young couple married, and he bore them a son, to whom he bequeathed his name. He won another scholarship, this time to pursue his PhD at Harvard, but not the money to take his new family with him. A separation occurred, and he returned to Africa to fulfill his promise to the continent. The mother and child stayed behind, but the bond of love survived the distances."

In that high-concept summation, the term "bequeathed" stands out. The Kenyan of the Luo tribe allegedly bequeathed his name but when Aunt Jane called from Nairobi in 1982, when the author was 21, she used the name "Barry," not the name on the cover of *Dreams from My Father*. To bequeath something implies an act of will, or an actual written will, but the account is short on documentation.

As the author explains, "there the album would close, and I would wander off content, swaddled in a tale that placed me in the center of a vast and orderly universe."

Like "myth," readers may find term "tale" of interest.

Of this storied African student, the author says, "Gramps might be struck by his resemblance to Nat King Cole, one of his favorite singers."

The author does not take the trouble to tell readers who, exactly, Gramps might be. He is Stanley Dunham, the author's white American grandfather. Gramps is not stating, "You know, this Kenyan student sure looks like Nat King Cole." The author is saying this is a comparison Gramps "might" make. But then, Gramps might not.

Nat King Cole (1919-1965) was a gifted jazz pianist, easily in Oscar Peterson's class, who became a hugely popular vocalist in the 1950s and 1960s, with a global following and a television show to boot. He passed away in 1965 but received a major revival in the early 1990s through his daughter Natalie's "Unforgettable" album. But contrary to what Gramps might say, Nat Cole bears little resemblance to the bespectacled, pipe-smoking African student who showed up at the University of Hawaii in 1959. *Dreams from My Father* does not include photos of the two men side by side, and, tellingly, no conventional photo section at all.

Stanley Dunham, the author's maternal grandfather, is an interesting fellow. Gramps is supposedly a humble furniture salesman but some scholars have spotted evidence of intelligence connections in his Army background. None of this emerges in *Dreams from My Father*, where Gramps is a homespun character something like "Grandpa" Amos McCoy played by Walter Brennan on "The Real McCoys."

Stanley Dunham passed away in 1992 but the author remembers him well. One day some tourists mistook his grandson for a Hawaiian, and Gramps told them "that boy happens to be my grandson, his mother is from Kansas, his father is from the interior of Kenya and there isn't an ocean for miles in either damn place."

Readers might note the precise recall in that statement. The author's mother and maternal grandfather have both validated the story, but readers can't double check with them because both are dead. Gramps, meanwhile, didn't worry about race and as the author explains:

"In the end I suppose that's what all the stories of my father were really about. They said less about the man himself than about the changes that had taken place in the people around him, the halting process by which my grandparents' racial attitudes had changed. The stories gave voice to a spirit that would grip the nation for that fleeting period between Kennedy's election and the passage of the Voting Rights Act."

So "the nation" is not Kenya but the United States. The stories about his father were "really" about "the seeming triumph of universalism over parochialism and narrowmindedness, a bright new world where differences of race or culture would instruct and amuse and perhaps ennoble. A useful fiction, one that haunts me no less than it haunted my family, evoking as it did some lost Eden that extends beyond mere childhood."

At this point the reader has heard some stories about the Kenyan father of the Luo tribe who met the shy, American girl in Russian class and the two fell in love. Now the author explains what all the stories were "really" about, and it has nothing to do with Africa or romance. It's all about the sixties in America, John Fitzgerald Kennedy, the Voting Rights Act, and some lost Eden. So readers might review a few things at this point.

Within the first 25 pages of *Dreams from My Father*, before the end of the "Origins" chapter, the author raises serious questions whether the voice in the book is his own. He has something to hide, and writes of a stubborn desire to protect himself from scrutiny. He tells readers why they are fully justified in not taking him at face value. In that short space, readers encounter "myth," "tales" and now the prospect of a "useful fiction."

Curious readers might check what the various presidential biographers, high-profile journalists and such had to say about a "useful fiction," and other openly evasive language, in what purports to be a factual and authentic biography of a politician. The author, of course, has more to explain on this theme.

"There was only one problem: My father was missing. He had left paradise, and nothing that my mother or grandparents told me could obviate that single, unassailable fact. Their stories didn't tell me why he had left. They couldn't describe what it might have been like had he stayed. Like the janitor, Mr. Reed, or the black girl who churned up dust as she raced down a Texas road, my father became a prop in someone else's narrative. An attractive prop – an alien with the heart of gold, the mysterious stranger who saves the town and wins the girl – but a prop nonetheless."

In a single paragraph of *Dreams from My Father*, the author uses "prop" three times. The father became "a prop in someone else's narrative," though the author did not identify the "someone else" who was spinning the narrative. The father was "an attractive prop" with his heart of gold and so forth, "but a prop nonetheless."

In this narrative, the father conducts a lot of multi-tasking. In the next paragraph the story gets better.

"I don't really blame my mother or grandparents for this," the author says. "My father may have preferred the image they created for him – indeed, he may have been complicit in its creation."

So he was more than a prop. He "may" have preferred the image created for him, and he "may" have been complicit in the myth his mother and grandparents created. That would be the tale, the useful fiction, and he may have wanted to be a prop in someone else's narrative. Readers can't get the Kenyan's opinion on that because at the time of writing, the early 1990s, he was dead. With his mother and grandfather also departed, readers have to take the narrator's word for everything, but he does attempt to document the Kenyan.

On Wednesday, June 20, 1962, the *Honolulu Star-Bulletin* published "Kenyan Student Wins Fellowship." The page-seven story with no byline reads:

> A University of Hawaii student, Barack H. Obama of Kenya, Africa, has been awarded a graduate faculty fellowship in economics at Harvard University.
>
> Obama, who began his studies at the university here three years ago, has been a straight "A" student. An economics major, he will study at Harvard for a Ph.D. in economics.
>
> He plans to return to Africa and work in economic development of underdeveloped areas and international trade at the planning and policy-making levels.
>
> A 1962 graduate, he leaves next week for a tour of Mainland universities before entering Harvard in the fall.

The article, of only 96 words, includes not a single quote from the Kenyan and nothing about meeting a shy American girl in Russian language class, falling in love, and getting married. That is the kind of story newspapers love, but readers find not a trace of it in the brief report.

Two days later, on Friday June 22, 1962, a reporter named John Griffin authored "First UH African Graduate Gives View on E-W Center," in the *Honolulu Advertiser*.

Dreams from My Father attempts to summarize the contents.

"In an article published in the *Honolulu Star-Bulletin*," the *Dreams* author says on page 26, "he appears guarded and responsible, the model student, ambassador for his continent. He mildly scolds the university for herding visiting students into dormitories and forcing them to attend programs designed to promote cultural understanding – a distraction, he says, from the practical training he seeks. Although he hasn't experienced any problems himself, he detects self-segregation and overt discrimination taking place between the various ethnic groups and expresses wry amusement at the fact that 'Caucasians' in Hawaii are occasionally at the receiving end of prejudice. But if his assessment is relatively clear-eyed, he is careful to end on a happy note: One thing other nations can learn from Hawaii, he said, is the willingness of races to work together toward common development, something he has found whites elsewhere too often unwilling to do."

A rather stern photo of the Kenyan accompanies the piece, more notable for what it does not contain. The Kenyan foreign student Barack Obama does not mention that during the course of his studies at the University of Hawaii he married an American student who bore his child. The Kenyan gives no indication that he planned to rejoin that wife and child in Hawaii before he returned to Kenya. After finishing Harvard, the Kenyan told Griffin, he planned to go home and enter "economic research, international trade or possibly politics."

The author of *Dreams from My Father* attempts to explain the omissions.

"I discovered this article, folded away among my birth certificate and old vaccination forms, when I was in high school. It's a short piece with a photograph of him. No mention is made of my mother and me, and I'm left to wonder whether the omission was intentional on my father's part, in anticipation of his long departure. Perhaps the reporter failed to ask personal questions, intimidated by my father's imperious manner; or perhaps it was an editorial decision, not part of the simple story that they were looking for. I wonder, too, whether the omission caused a fight between my parents."

The author attributes the absence of his parents in the story to a lapse by the reporter. In other words, he blames the media. Maybe the couple was "not part of the simple story they were looking for." On the other hand, maybe the article is not the complex story the author was looking for.

A photo of the June 22 article as printed would have made an illustration of some consequence, particularly with the picture of the Kenyan student Barack Obama. So would the birth certificate the author says he found with the article. Why he didn't already have his birth certificate, or why it was tucked away with some press clippings and vaccination records, is not explained. *Dreams from My Father* contains no photo of the birth certificate, nor any documents confirming that the African Barack Obama, the Kenyan foreign student of unsurpassed concentration, is indeed the father as a matter of unassailable fact. Such documentation has remained elusive, along with much other material pertaining to the president.

"Barack is such a beautiful name."

The author (page 30) charts the time they lived in Indonesia, "the result of my mother's marriage to an Indonesian named Lolo, another student she met at the University of Hawaii." The author does not provide Lolo's surname, Soetoro, but explains that his first name meant "crazy" in Hawaiian, which the author says amused Gramps no end. Lolo Soetoro passed away in 1987 in Jakarta, so readers won't be able to get the stepfather's take on that, the Kenyan, or anything else.

The author's mother, who calls him "Barry," had a faith "she refused to describe as religious." In fact, her experience told her it was "sacrilegious." It was "a faith that rational, thoughtful people could shape their own destiny... She was a lonely witness for secular humanism, a soldier for the New Deal, Peace Corps, position-paper liberalism." Further, "She had only one ally in all this, and that was the distant authority of my father." This father is not Lolo Soetoro the Indonesian student his mother actually married. It's the elusive Kenyan, the prop in someone else's narrative.

"Increasingly she would remind me of his story, how he had grown up poor, in a poor country, in a poor continent," with a life as hard as anything Lolo might have known. According to his mother, "he had led his life according to principles that demanded a different kind of toughness, principles that promised a higher form of power." Here the profile escalates sharply.

According to his mother, this tough Kenyan lived by "principles that promised a higher form of power," but the author fails to name a single one. More troubling is this "higher form of power" these principles promise. Higher than what? one might wonder, and to whom, exactly, do the principles promise the power? And over whom do they exercise it? The author also fails to note where these power arrangements might be operating anywhere in the world. Readers can't be blamed for catching a whiff of megalomania here. They might take the time to see what presidential biographers, PBS documentarians, establishment journalists and such said about this mysterious "higher form of power." Determinism also appears to be in play, as on page 50:

"I would follow his example, my mother decided. I had no choice. It was all in the genes."

So his mother, who corrected all the accounts about the father, made the call. Like Gramps, readers might note that this author shows not a trace of the rebellion that prompted millions of other young people to rebel against the political and social views of their parents, and to defy their parents' plans for their career in favor of their own. The author of *Dreams from My Father*, on the other hand, is utterly obedient and unquestioning. The decision was on his mother, that shy American girl who fell for the Kenyan student in Russian language class. Beyond the genetic determinism, readers get some physical details.

"You have me to thank for your eyebrows," the mother says, "your father has these little wispy eyebrows that don't amount to much. But your brains, your character, you got from him."

So it's in the genes and it's all about the father. Had a photo of the Kenyan been included, readers could have verified that his eyebrows were not exactly wispy. And despite what Gramps might have thought, the Kenyan does not look like Nat King Cole. This author, who has a stubborn desire to protect himself from scrutiny, does not trust readers to assess a key character's appearance for themselves.

Meanwhile, back in Hawaii, the author gets into the prestigious Punahou school, the finest in Hawaii, explaining on page 58, "I was considered only because of the intervention of Gramps's boss, who was an alumnus." So his admission had nothing to do with stellar grades, and as the author explains, "my first experience with affirmative action, it seems, had little to do with race."

The author does not name Gramps' influential boss, and never devotes much attention to what Gramps himself does for a living. The author is clearly well connected and the family is not exactly hurting financially. At the Punahou school other revelations ensue.

"I thought your name was Barry," says homeroom teacher, Miss Hefty.

"Would you prefer we called you Barry?"

Readers have already learned that Aunt Jane was using "Barry" in her 1982 telephone call, when the author was 21, to announce the Kenyan father's death. In this scene, long before he turned 21, the student has something else in mind.

"Barack is such a beautiful name," says Miss Hefty, whose first name, Mabel, is not provided.

"Your grandfather tells me your father is Kenyan. I used to live in Kenya, you know. Teaching children just your age. It's such a magnificent country. Do you know what tribe your father is from?" The ten-year-old said "Luo." He is up on it. A redheaded girl wanted to touch his hair and "a ruddy-faced boy asked me if my father ate people." At home, Gramps says, "isn't it terrific that Miss Hefty used to live in Kenya?"

Later in the school year, the student addresses some boys at lunch.

"My grandfather, see, he's a chief," he says. "It's sort of like the king of the tribe, you know... Like the Indians. So that makes my father a prince. He'll take over when my grandfather dies."

As the author explains, "a part of me really began to believe the story. But another part of me knew that what I was telling them was a lie, something I'd constructed from the scraps of information I'd picked up from my mother."

So by page 63 the author has added "lie" to such terms as "myth," "tale," "useful fiction," and "prop." And the author says he preferred the father's more distant image, "an image I could alter on a whim or ignore when convenient."

This guy can be anything the author wants him to be, and readers have good cause to wonder about that. At the same time, the father "remained something unknown," even though his mother had explained about his hard life in a poor continent, his principles that promised a higher form of power, and how he got his brains and character from him. The mother had also explained how it was in his genes that he would follow him, and that he had no choice in the matter.

The author's mother had maintained a correspondence with the distant father throughout the time they had been in Indonesia, and "he knew all about me." Like his mother, his father had remarried, "and I now had five brothers and one sister living in Kenya."

So the Kenyan Barack H. Obama had, count 'em, six children. As readers can imagine, with that kind of responsibility, bolting for Hawaii to visit the American woman who bore his child must have been quite an operation, especially since the woman was now married to the Indonesian Lolo Soetoro. Even so, the father was coming to Hawaii to visit – for a full month.

"He was much thinner than I expected," the author (page 65) explains, "the bones of his knees cutting the legs of his trousers in sharp angles." The Kenyan wore a blue blazer, white shirt and a scarlet ascot. There was "a fragility about his frame" and he carried a cane with a "blunt ivory head." When he took off his horned-rimmed glasses the eyes are yellow, "the eyes of someone who has had malaria more than once."

Lots of color and detail here, and medical knowledge on malaria, but readers may find the character something of a composite. The blue, white and red clothing evokes the Union Jack or American stars and stripes more than any sort of African style. No mention here of Gramps saying the fellow looked like Nat King Cole. The Kenyan gave his son three wooden figurines "a lion, an elephant and an ebony man in tribal dress beating a drum," all items commonly purchased by tourists. The Kenyan explains, "they are only small things." Maybe he meant that his son could expect bigger and more meaningful things during the month-long visit.

"There was so much to tell in that single month, so much explaining to do; and yet, when I reach back into my memory for the words of my father, the small interactions or conversations we might have had, they seem irretrievably lost."

People who knew the Kenyan Barack Obama consistently describe him as verbose and opinionated. Here the author can't remember a single statement this big-time talker made during an entire month. It was all "irretrievably lost," like those 18 minutes on the Nixon tapes or a batch of Hillary Clinton's emails.

Coming so soon after the author added "lie" to "myth" and other evasive language, readers had grounds to believe that this too was part of that "useful fiction," a mere prop in someone else's narrative, as the author also said. He can't explain the irretrievable loss, but his wife, here unnamed, says boys and their fathers don't always have much to say to each other unless and until they trust. Indeed, the author says, "I often felt mute before him, and he never pushed me to speak." That part the author remembers, along with the yellow eyes of someone who had malaria more than once.

Before he departed back to Africa, the father was coming to speak in Miss Hefty's fifth-grade class.

"We have a special treat for you today," Miss Hefty says. "Barry Obama's father is here, and he's come all the way from Kenya, in Africa, to tell us all about his country."

In the style of Gramps, readers might note that Miss Hefty, who has already proclaimed "Barack is such a beautiful name," is now using the Obama surname, the one on the cover of *Dreams from My Father*. She is not using Soetoro, which was in fact the surname of the Indonesian student his mother had married. The narrator of this tale is inserting the Kenyan's names in an incremental fashion.

On this theme, readers might check out "A Kid Named Barry," the cover story of the Spring 2007 issue of the *Punahou Bulletin*. Author Carlyn Tani, a 1969 Punahou alum, refers to Ann Soetoro, and says that Mabel Hefty "would sometimes pull Barry aside after class and tell him stories about her experiences in Kenya." She quotes another teacher, Pal Eldredge, who says "Barry was a happy kid." Tani was not present when the Kenyan himself visited the Mabel Hefty's class. Here is how the appearance went down, according to the author, on page 69:

"He was leaning against Miss Hefty's thick oak desk and describing the deep gash in the earth where mankind had first appeared. He spoke of the wild animals that still roamed the plains, the tribes that still required a young boy to kill a lion to prove his manhood. He spoke of the customs of the Luo, how elders received the utmost respect and make laws for all to follow under great-trunked trees. And he told us of Kenya's struggle to be free, how the British had wanted to stay and unjustly rule the people, just as they had in America; how many had been enslaved only because of the color of their skin, just as they had in America, but that Kenyans, like all of us in the room, longed to be free and develop themselves through hard work and sacrifice."

Like the four-paragraph article in the *Honolulu Star-Bulletin*, the account includes not a single direct quotation from the man the author described to his pals at the prestigious Punahou school. After his father spoke, Miss Hefty was "absolutely beaming with pride" and classmates asked his father questions, "each of which my father appeared to consider carefully before answering." The author gives no detail on the questions, perhaps about that deep gash in the earth where mankind first appeared, or his father's answers.

Carlyn Tani's 2007 "A Kid Named Barry" article includes no quotations from Miss Hefty about the visit. Born in 1915, she started teaching at Punahou in 1947, retiring in 1980. Mabel Hefty died in 1995, the same year *Dreams from My Father* appeared, so she probably didn't perform any correcting in the style of the author's mother. Readers have to take author's word for everything, but as he said, "I don't fault people their suspicions."

Meanwhile, the *Honolulu Star-Bulletin* had seen fit to note the Kenyan's departure from the islands for Harvard in 1962. Ten years later, the scholarly Kenyan makes a triumphant return to address his American son's class at the prestigious Punahou school. As any journalist or editor would recognize, that's a great story and the *Honolulu Star-Bulletin* would have been all over it. This would have been a feature, with plenty of photos, but apparently the major newspaper in the Hawaiian Islands, and mainland dailies such as the *Los Angeles Times*, showed no interest at all. Perhaps that was the fault of the same reporter who failed to mention the author and his mother in 1962. As with so much else, all the information in this account is from the author alone.

"You've got a pretty impressive father," a certain Mr. Eldridge explains. That could be a reference to Pal Eldredge, a Punahou teacher.

"A Teacher's Hefty Influence," a July 29, 2007 *Honolulu Star-Bulletin* article by Susan Essoyan, says that Eldredge was present for the Kenyan's talk but, curiously, the recently retired teacher had nothing to say about it to the reporter.

In the author's account, the ruddy-faced boy who had asked about cannibalism said "your dad is pretty cool," a direct quote. That raises another issue, especially for journalists.

Note that the author has plenty of direct quotes from Gramps, grandma Toot, and others, but not a single quote from the time his Kenyan father showed up in the classroom of Miss Hefty, a teacher who had lived in Kenya. Any kid of ten would tend to remember a thing like that, but maybe this too was irretrievably lost.

In the next two weeks, the author says, father and son posed for pictures, "the only ones I have of us together, me holding an orange basketball, his gift to me, him showing off the tie I've bought him." No word about the pipe the author says he bought him for his birthday, but the tie prompts the Kenyan to say, "Ah, people will know that I am very important wearing such a tie." That's a direct quote, so maybe all the memories of the visit are not irretrievably lost after all. The author managed to retrieve at least one. On the other hand, maybe the photos are lost because neither one shows up in *Dreams from My Father*, which has no photo section. Like Gramps, readers might wonder about that. Readers might see what the authoritative presidential biographers had to say about that, and check if those photos showed up anywhere else.

As the author has it, father and son go to a Dave Brubeck concert, of which the son (page 70) provides no details of personnel, venue, or compositions performed. Actually, the concert, like a lot of material in this book, might have an existential problem. The classic Dave Brubeck quartet with Paul Desmond, Joe Morello and Eugene Wright disbanded at the end of 1967. The author is writing about 1971, when Brubeck lost his recording contract with Columbia, not exactly the ticket to extensive touring. Brubeck had suffered an injury diving in the surf in Hawaii but that was way back in 1951.

On the other hand, the Kenyan student would be unlikely to have much knowledge of jazz, "an American musical art form" as Jazz Messengers drummer Art Blakey said, after living for a time in Africa. "No America, no jazz," Blakey said. "I've seen people try to connect it to other countries, for instance to Africa, but it doesn't have a damn thing to do with Africa."

Meanwhile, on the day of the Kenyan's departure, as the author and his mother help him pack his bags, "he unearthed two records, forty-fives, in dull brown dust jackets."

"Barry! Look here," the Kenyan says. "I forgot that I had brought these for you. The sounds of your continent."

Miss Hefty, readers might recall, already said "Barack is such a beautiful name," but the Kenyan is sticking to "Barry." So the African father, who worked with "unsurpassed concentration" and graduated at the top of his class in three years, also suffers from some memory issues. Maybe he forgot that he "bequeathed" his own name to the American. He also forgot to give his son Barry the 45-RPM records upon arrival, when he gave him the wooden carvings of the lion, elephant, and the ebony man in tribal dress beating a drum. And according to the narrative, he even failed to break out the records at Christmas. Perhaps to compensate, he now fires up the family's old stereo. The music wasn't "Take Five," "Giant Steps," or any jazz composition. It was good old rock and roll.

"A tinny guitar lick opened," the author writes, "then the sharp horns, the thump of drums, then the guitar again, and then the voices, clean and joyful as they rode up the back beat, urging us on." The author fails to name the tune or identify the recording artists. Kids tend to remember things like that, but maybe it was irretrievably lost.

"Come, Barry," the father said. "You will learn from the master." And "suddenly his slender body was swaying back and forth" and, the author says, "I took my first tentative steps."

It was like something from "American Bandstand," and readers had a right to wonder what, exactly, was going on. The pipe-puffing yellow-eyed African, who looked frail and carried a cane, was suddenly transformed into a cross between Chubby Checker and Edwin Starr's Agent Double-O Soul. But then, the author is already on record that for his father he preferred "an image I could alter on a whim or ignore when convenient."

The Kenyan had a lot to say in John Griffin's June 22, 1962 *Honolulu Advertiser* article, but the author had no quotes from the Kenyan's appearance in Miss Hefty's class. Over a full month with his father, the man of unsurpassed concentration from whom he got his brains and his character, he can't remember a single thing the Kenyan said. It's all irretrievably lost, except it isn't.

The author is at pains to tell the reader that father and son went to a Dave Brubeck concert. And he remembers what his father told the son about "the sounds of your continent" and how the master hoofer boogied about the room on the day he departed back to Africa, from whence he came.

If readers find this strange, they might recall that the African was a prop in someone else's narrative, altered or ignored as the occasion demands. Interactions they "might" have had over an entire month are irretrievably lost – gone forever. The author talks up the myth, the tale, the prop, the lie, and the useful fiction. He says people have trouble taking him at face value and confirms that their suspicions are justified. That does not exactly evoke the "granite slab of truth" the author was touting.

On the other hand, *Dreams from My Father,* a book of 442 pages, gives readers much more to ponder. For example, on page 76 readers meet "a poet named Frank who lived in a dilapidated house in a run-down section of Waikiki."

"They'll drive you to drink, boy."

As the narrator explains, Frank "had enjoyed some modest notoriety once, was a contemporary of Richard Wright and Langston Hughes during his years in Chicago –Gramps once showed me some of his work anthologized in a book of black poetry. But by the time I met Frank he must have been pushing eighty, with a big dewlapped face and an ill-kempt gray Afro that made him look like an old, shaggy lion."

The author who has that stubborn desire to protect himself from scrutiny provides no last name for Frank, but that presents no problem. In a televised September 20, 1995 speech at the Cambridge library, readily available on the Internet, the future U.S. Senator from Illinois and President of the United States clearly identified the poet as "Frank Marshall Davis." As it happens, Davis did enjoy more than modest notoriety.

In *Livin' the Blues: Memoirs of a Black Journalist and Poet* (University of Wisconsin Press, 1992), a fascinating read, Davis proudly notes his inclusion in *Who's Who in the Midwest* and *Who's Who in America*. In this book, Frank (page 276 *et environs*) is completely candid about being a Communist, and makes it clear that he joined the Communist Party after the Hitler-Stalin Pact when many others departed, never to return. Davis joined a white-led party that did not regard blacks as Americans and had mapped out a separate homeland for blacks in the south.

Frank contended that genuine Communists had one principle in common, to abolish racism. In that claim, Frank appears to have glossed over a few things. For example, in a letter to Engels, Karl Marx his own self described German Socialist Ferdinand Lassalle as a "Jewish nigger," adding:

"It is now perfectly clear to me that, as testified also by his cranial formation and hair growth, he is descended from the negroes who joined Moses exodus from Egypt, unless his paternal mother or grandmother was crossed with a nigger. Well this combination of Jewish and German stock with the negroid basic substances is bound to yield a strange product. The fellow's importunity is also nigger-like."

Marx was also a believer in phrenology, quackery that extrapolates a person's character from the shape of the skull. Note his reference to "cranial formation."

Frank's belief that genuine Communists sought to abolish racism invites a comparison with the account of a black man who actually lived in the Soviet Union.

Robert Robinson, author of *Black on Red: My 44 Years Inside the Soviet Union*, viewed Communism as (page 434) "a system of government that views freedom as a threat to its existence." Robinson (page 15), "observed their system not as a white idealist but as a black man who had been well trained by racism in America to judge the sincerity of a person's words and deeds. I can say as an expert that one of the greatest myths ever launched by the Kremlin's propaganda apparatus is that Soviet society is free from racism."

That was indeed the contention of Frank Marshall Davis, who was part of that propaganda apparatus.

"Knowing also that Russia had no colonies," Davis wrote in *Livin' the Blues* (page 277) "and was strongly opposed to the imperialism under which my black kinsmen lived in Africa, and that those American forces which most staunchly resisted our own demands for equality were the most rabid foes of Russia, I concluded the Soviet Union held the same position internationally that blacks were in domestically. Russians were looked upon as the niggers of the globe."

The belief that Russia had no colonies would come as a surprise to inmates of the many non-Russian nations Russia conquered and ruled. Curious readers might also try to find other writers, black or white, who believe that Russians were looked upon as the "niggers of the globe."

According to Robinson, (page 301), "all non-Russians are considered inferior," with blacks ranking at the bottom and treated "as second-class human beings." In 1962 "race prejudice against blacks reached a fever pitch," wrote Robinson, "worse than anything I recalled in the United States during the 1920s and without question worse than in the United States after the decade of the 1950s." Every black person Robinson knew in the USSR was "painfully aware of Soviet racism."

Robinson was a skilled toolmaker and inventor but official letters came addressed to (page 311) "Negro Robert Robinson."

The author of *Dreams for My Father* explains that Frank was a contemporary of Richard Wright. Frank actually knew Wright rather well and called him "Dick." In *Livin' the Blues*, Frank says (page 243) that, "as a writer, he is by far the most powerful yet produced in black America." Davis read the galley proofs for *Native Son* and reviewed *Black Boy* for the Associated Negro Press (ANP). Wright used the photo Davis had taken of him to accompany the *Time* magazine review of *Black Boy*.

Richard Wright joined the Communist Party through the John Reed Clubs, to which Frank devotes some attention in *Livin' the Blues*. Unlike Frank, Wright did not remain a Communist.

"I was not surprised when Wright quit the Communist Party," Frank explained. Frank accused Dick of selling out and of "redbaiting," which apparently applies to any criticism of Communism. But in Frank's view, Wright "was still a Marxist" who had "merely quit the organization and dumped his former comrades, not the ideology." Actually, Richard Wright had dumped it all, as he explained in his contribution to *The God That Failed*, the anti-Communist classic from 1949.

Wright discovered that in the Communist Party, dominated by whites, "a man could not have his say." Party bosses derided the black American writer as a "bastard intellectual" and "incipient Trotskyite" with an "anti-leadership attitude." The Communist Party, Wright wrote, "felt it had to assassinate me morally merely because I did not want to be bound by its decisions," adding, "I knew that if they held state power I should have been declared guilty of treason and my execution would have followed." Wright was right about that, and faithful Frank would have approved the sentence.

Joining Wright in *The God That Failed* were writers such as Andre

Gide, author of *The Immoralist* and winner of the Nobel Prize for literature in 1947. The friends of the Soviet Union, Gide wrote, refused to see anything bad there, "so it happens that truth is spoken with hatred and falsehood with love."

Arthur Koestler wrote *Darkness at Noon*, the book CPUSA members like Frank were not supposed to read. Koestler joined the Communist Party at the age of 26 but what he experienced in the USSR disturbed him. He saw the ravages of the Ukraine famine and noticed that in the USSR people disappeared. "At no time and in no country," Koestler wrote in *The God That Failed*, "have more revolutionaries been killed and reduced to slavery than in Soviet Russia." When Koestler parted company with Communism he too was attacked, but after Stalin signed his pact with the Nazi regime, "I no longer cared whether Hitler's allies called me a counter-revolutionary."

Readers won't find any of this in *Dreams from My Father* but the book does make it clear that Frank was active in Chicago, where he served as a journalistic Stakhanov. Frank was a board-certified Communist and might be called an "Uncle Joe" because whatever Josef Stalin wanted, Davis wanted too. In that cause he was not alone. Anna Louise Strong, a white American Communist who wrote for the *Atlantic* and other high-profile publications, opined in her book *I Change Worlds* that "one must not make a god of Stalin. He was too important for that." Frank wasn't quite as poetic about the Soviet dictator, but Frank's work for the *Chicago Star* followed the Communist Party line in politically correct perfection.

In Chicago, Davis worked with Vernon Jarrett of the Council of American Youth for Democracy, a Communist Party front group and a kind of Stalin Youth chapter. Frank also worked with Jarrett on the Citizens Committee to Aid Packinghouse Workers. Frank served on the board of the Chicago Civil Liberties Committee with his fellow Stalinist Paul Robeson and a man named Robert R. Taylor. None of this gets any ink in *Dreams from My Father*, and neither does the reason Frank, who enjoyed all that notoriety in Chicago, suddenly moved to Hawaii.

The Communist Party USA was a wholly owned subsidiary of the

Soviet Union and like all national Communist parties managed through the Communist International, the Comintern, in Moscow. The trouble with Henry Wallace, the Communist-backed candidate for president in 1948, insiders used to quip, was that he confused the common man with the Comintern. Party members lived under strict discipline, and like the inmates of Communist nations, they were not at liberty to do their own thing.

In 1948, the Party shipped Davis to Hawaii, not yet a state and a major target of Stalin's post-war expansionism. In that cause, Frank wrote for *Honolulu Record*, a publication backed by the CPUSA and the International Longshoremen's and Warehousemen's Union, headed by Harry Bridges, another Communist and Soviet agent. Davis' journalism was the same pro-Soviet boilerplate. He blasted opponents as fascists, racists, Ku Kluckers, Nazi storm troopers and so on. His primary political targets were Democrats, particularly U.S. President Harry Truman.

Frank Marshall Davis was a photography enthusiast and in his first year in Hawaii he deployed a telephoto lens to take shots of remote Hawaiian beaches. So it was not for nothing that Davis wound up on the FBI's Security Index. This meant that in the event of war he would have been arrested immediately. Frank Marshall Davis' FBI file runs 600 pages, longer than *Dreams from My Father* and *Livin' the Blues*, and was only made available in recent times. Curious readers might chart how Frank comes across in the accounts of presidential biographers, establishment journalists, PBS documentarians and such, if he shows up at all.

The CPUSA organization in the islands was formidable but ultimately lost the battle. President Dwight Eisenhower signed the Hawaii Admission Act on March 12, 1959 and on August 21, 1959, Hawaii duly became the fiftieth state. The Party kept Frank on location, a decision of great significance.

If Frank was only the president's "mentor," as Paul Kengor contends, one doubts whether he would have been included in *Dreams from My Father*. As Kengor notes, Ronald Reagan and Hillary Clinton did not write much about their own mentors. In contrast, Frank was very important to the author, who also has this stubborn desire to avoid scrutiny. So no surprise that the author decks out the Stalinist Davis in a disguise like the jocular Grady Wilson on "Sanford and Son," the kind of happy-go-lucky stereotype Communist Party activists hated.

Frank, says the author on page 77, "would read us his poetry whenever we stopped by his house, sharing whiskey with Gramps out of an emptied jelly jar. As the night wore on the two of them would solicit my help in composing dirty limericks. Eventually the conversation would turn to laments about women."

The author does not include any of Frank's poems, nor the jointly composed dirty limericks. As for the laments about women:

"They'll drive you to drink, boy," Frank would say, "and if you let 'em, they'll drive you into your grave."

Unlike the Kenyan, readers might note, nothing about Frank seems irretrievably lost to the author, who never hesitates to quote him directly and is obviously very fond of the man. With the Kenyan father, the author preferred a distant image he "could alter on a whim or ignore altogether." In similar style, the author ignores Frank's faithful service on behalf of the Soviet Union. *Dreams from My Father* includes no selections or even quotes from Frank's journalism, a huge body of work reflecting his belief that the white European Stalinists who ran the Soviet Union were always right and represented the future. Curious readers might explore how many other writers of the time, black and white, held similar views.

In *Livin' the Blues*, Frank Marshall Davis wrote extensively about jazz and taught jazz history at the Communist Party's Abraham Lincoln School in Chicago. Davis was not a musician and held some rather strange ideas. For example, he called be-bop an effort to make jazz "acceptable to traditional white standards." Actually, the be-boppers, all virtuoso musicians, wanted to play something that was interesting to themselves, and outside of the traditional musical structures.

Frank also worked as a disc jockey playing jazz on WJJD, a radio station owned by the multi-millionaire Marshall Field. This is not revealed in *Dreams from My Father*, which tellingly attributes affection for jazz to the Kenyan student. In this tale it was the African, not Frank, who allegedly took his ten-year-old son to a Dave Brubeck concert and danced around the house as though auditioning for "Soul Train." Like Gramps, readers might recall that the African was a prop in someone else's narrative, part of the author's myth and useful fiction.

"Respect came from what you did and not who your daddy was."

On page 79 of *Dreams from My Father* the author claims he played basketball well enough to take his game to university courts. There other black men, has-beens and gym rats among them, would teach him an attitude that had nothing to do with sport, "that respect came from what you did and not who your daddy was." Given the author's stubborn need to avoid scrutiny, the useful fiction about the Kenyan, and the camouflaging of Frank, that is surely more than a throwaway line. In someone else's narrative, nothing appears by accident and everything has a purpose. It doesn't matter who your daddy was, readers are to understand. The author's daddy was important, but not his only influence.

He goes to the library and reads James Baldwin, Ralph Ellison, Langston Hughes, Richard Wright, and W.E.B. DuBois. He finds all of them "exhausted, bitter men, the devil at their heels," a remarkable statement given that Frank had described Richard Wright as the most powerful writer black America had produced. James Baldwin was also a contender with his 1963 bestseller *The Fire Next Time* and other books.

For the author of *Dreams from My Father*, "only Malcolm X's autobiography seemed to offer something different." One line in the book stayed with him, Malcolm's wish that the white blood that ran through him "might be expunged." That would never "recede into mere abstraction" like all that stuff about blue-eyed devils. So the author wonders "what else I would be severing if and when I left my mother and my grandparents at some uncharted border." So in this narrative, the legacy problem is not the Frank the Stalinist poet. It's the white folks in his background.

The author and his friend Ray meet a tall, gaunt man named Malik, a follower of the Nation of Islam. As readers may know, this group holds that a scientist named Yakub created the white race more than 6,000 years ago on the Isle of Patmos. According to this racist belief, which is not part of Islam, Shakespeare, Tolstoy, Eleanor Roosevelt, Johann Sebastian Bach, Abraham Lincoln, Hillary Clinton, Elton John, Gramps and the author's own mother all proceed from Yakub's experiment. Like Gramps, readers might find it hard to track down scholars, statesmen and writers who take this seriously.

Dreams of My Father gives no clue what the author thinks about Yakub. Maybe the author knew all about him then forgot it. After all, as readers have seen, he claims to have forgotten everything a verbose Kenyan said during an entire a month. Gramps might say the author lacks courage and is not much of a critical thinker.

"Malcolm tells it like it is, no doubt about it," says one of the guys who overheard the author conversing with Malik. This prompts another unidentified "guy" to say:

"Yeah, but I tell you what. You won't see me moving to no African jungle anytime soon. Or some goddamned desert somewhere, sitting on a carpet with a bunch of Arabs. And you won't see me stop eating no ribs. Gotta have them ribs. And pussy, too. Don't Malcolm talk about no pussy? Now you know that ain't gonna work."

As he drives to the hoop, Ray says "I don't need no books telling me how to be black."

The author gets back to Frank, "sitting in his overstuffed chair, a book of poetry in his lap, his reading glasses slipping down his nose. It had been three years, the author says but "he looked the same, his mustache a little whiter, dangling like dead ivy over his heavy upper lip, his cut-off jeans with a few more holes and tied at the waist with a length of rope."

Frank pulls down a bottle of whiskey and pours drinks into plastic cups. The conversation centers on conditions back in Kansas, where both Frank and Gramps lived, and where Frank says he would have to step off the sidewalk to let the white folks pass by. Gramps would not be eager to talk about that, and he can't know Frank the way Frank knows him. Meanwhile, Grandma Toot had evidently been frightened by a large black man, and Frank explains the dynamic.

"What I'm trying to tell you is, your grandma's right to be scared. She's at least as right as Stanley is. She understands that black people have a reason to hate. That's just how it is. For your sake, I wish it were otherwise. But it's not. So you might as well get used to it."

Readers might note that Stanley and grandma Toot both validate this "reason to hate." Meanwhile:

"Frank closed his eyes again. His breathing slowed until he seemed to be asleep. I thought about waking him, then decided against it and walked back to the car. The earth shook under my feet, ready to crack open at any moment. I stopped, trying to steady myself, and knew for the first time that I was utterly alone." Except he wasn't alone. His mother and maternal grandparents were still around, and so was Frank.

In this myth, tale, and useful fiction, "black people have a reason to hate." That squares with Davis, a prodigious hater, and the Communist Party (CPUSA) to which he belonged is a hate group by any standard. Frank offers more lessons when the author is about to head to the mainland for college. The author fails to note that Frank studied journalism at Friends College then transferred to Kansas State, so he did not lack educational opportunity and took full advantage. In this tale, however, Frank warns that college is "an advanced degree in compromise."

"Well, that's the problem, isn't it? You *don't know*. You're just like the rest of these young cats out here. All you know is that college is the next thing you're supposed to do. And the people who are old enough to know better, who fought all those years for your right to go to college – they're just so happy to see you in there that they won't tell you the truth. The real price of admission."

"And what's that?"

"Leaving your race at the door. Leaving your people behind. Understand something, boy. You're not going to college to get educated. You're going there to get trained. They'll train you to want what you don't need. They'll train you to manipulate words so they don't mean anything anymore. They'll train you to forget what it is that you already know. They'll train you so good, you'll start believing what they tell you about equal opportunity and the American way and all that shit. They'll give you a corner office and invite you to fancy dinners, and tell you you're a credit to your race. Until you want to actually start running things, and they'll yank on your chain and let you know that you may be a well-trained, well-paid nigger, but you're a nigger just the same."

So should he go to college?

Frank's shoulders slumped, and he fell back in his chair with a sigh.

"No, I didn't say that. You've got to go. I'm just telling you to keep your eyes open. Stay awake."

"It made me smile," the author writes, "thinking back on Frank and his old Black Power dashiki self. In some ways, he was as incurable as my mother, as certain in his faith, living in the same sixties time warp that Hawaii had created."

Readers might recall that when the Kenyan was about to return to Africa, the author decked him out in American influence with "the music of your continent." Now Frank, the card-playing, whiskey-drinking jokester who fancies himself a sage, shows the African influence as "his old Black Power dashiki self." Frank can't be ignored, but like the Kenyan he can be altered on a whim. In someone else's narrative, which is also a myth and a tale, pretty much anything goes.

The Kenyan Barack Obama did not think for a moment that a college education involved compromise or somehow selling out his race. Indeed, he jumped at the chance to attend the University of Hawaii, and that raises another issue. If Barack Obama's American son chose the University of Hawaii, that would have been quite a story for the *Honolulu Star-Bulletin*, which noted the Kenyan's departure for Harvard.

In this tale, young Barry shows no inclination whatsoever to follow the educational footsteps of the Kenyan. Instead he is off to Occidental College, an upscale private liberal arts school in Los Angeles. No word whether, as with the prestigious Punahou school, family connections were the primary factor in admission. The narrator mentions no academic scholarship.

Occidental College put out the literary magazine *Feast*, and in the Spring 1982 issue the student from Hawaii known as Barry published a poem titled "Pop," in which the subject "recites an old poem he wrote before his mother died." So "Pop" is a poet, and as the student has it:

Pop takes another shot, neat,
Points out the same amber
Stain on his shorts that I've got on mine and
Makes me smell his smell, coming
From me...

The "Pop" poem concludes:

I see my face, framed within
Pop's black-framed glasses
And know he's laughing too.

In *Dreams from My Father*, the narrator never calls the Kenyan "Pop." This is clearly Frank, a poet, and the author sees his own face framed within Pop's black-framed glasses. The author has amber stains on his shorts, just like Pop, who "makes me smell his smell, coming from me." What that might mean, exactly, invites speculation, but as readers can see it's all rather intimate and personal. Stanley Dunham was still around when the poem appeared, but Gramps is not on record with any interpretation of the work. Neither did Toot or the author's mother publish her thoughts on the "Pop" poem, which nowhere appears in *Dreams from My Father*. The author, after all, has a stubborn desire to protect himself from scrutiny. On the other hand, at that point the student's influences were certainly showing.

In the accounts of Occidental students and professors alike, the student Barry Soetoro was a doctrinaire pro-Soviet Marxist, and readers might wonder where that came from. The obvious source is "Pop," also known as Frank, not the African student of unsurpassed concentration.

Though not productive as a writer, the Kenyan Barack Obama authored "Problems of Our Socialism," in the July 1965 issue of *East Africa Journal*. He is a man of the left, making a case for communal ownership, nationalization and such.

As Barry Rubin notes in *Silent Revolution: How the Left Rose to Political Power and Cultural Dominance*, the Kenyan wanted to tax citizens on the basis of wealth and race. Non-blacks were "interlopers who essentially had no rights," so the Kenyan was not exactly inclusive and a believer in diversity. He clearly wanted a statist government and a planned society but his views were Kenya-centric, a kind of national socialism. As Rubin notes, Barack Obama "rejected old-style Marxism and Communism." In his paper for *East Africa Journal*, the Kenyan wrote "one can choose to develop by the bootstraps rather than become a pawn to some foreign powers such Sekou Toure did." Toure was president of Guinea, and in 1961 he expelled the Soviet ambassador and accused the Soviets of plotting to overthrow him.

If the Kenyan Barack Obama had been pro-Soviet, he would have welcomed such a move and championed the all-white Soviet dictatorship. And if the Kenyan had in fact been pro-Soviet, his first choice for college would have been Patrice Lumumba University in the USSR, the socialist motherland, not the University of Hawaii in the capitalist United States. Frank, on the other hand, was a pro-Soviet propagandist who believed that the all-white Soviet dictatorship was always right. And Frank never waivered from that belief.

At Oxy, as he called it, "to avoid being mistaken for a sellout," the student Barry hangs out with Marxist professors and the politically active black students. Fellow student Marcus has a run-in with the LAPD.

"They had no reason to stop me. No reason 'cept I was walking in a white neighborhood. Made me spread-eagle against the car. One of 'em pulled out his piece. I didn't let 'em scare me, though. That's what gets these storm troopers off, seeing fear in a black man." The author had been "listening to Marcus pronounce on his authentic black experience." Marcus also tells "Barack" that *Heart of Darkness* is a "racist tract" that will "poison your mind." A black student named Regina, also without a last name, witnesses the exchange (page 104).

"What did Marcus call you just now? Some African name, wasn't it?"
"Barack."
"I thought your name was Barry."
"Barack's my given name. My father's name. He was Kenyan."

"Does it mean something?"

"It means 'blessed.' In Arabic. My grandfather was a Muslim."

"Barack, it's beautiful," Regina says, in the style of Miss Hefty, the Punahou teacher who had been to Kenya. But Regina is curious.

"So why does everybody call you Barry?"

"Habit, I guess. My father used it when he arrived in the States. I don't know whether that was his idea or somebody else's. He probably used Barry because it was easier to pronounce. You know – helped him to fit in. Then it got passed on to me. So I could fit in."

Like Gramps, readers might have a hard time finding cases where the Kenyan calls himself "Barry." Earlier in the narrative, when the author explained that the Kenyan from the Luo tribe "bequeathed" his name, there was no mention of "Barry." But then, as the author says, this is someone who can be altered on a whim or ignored when convenient, the familiar prop in someone else's narrative.

The Kenyan prop would surface again during the author's first summer in New York, when his mother and sister stop for a visit. They go see *Black Orpheus*, allegedly the first movie she had seen, at age 16 when she was working as an au pair in Chicago, "the first time that I'd ever been really on my own."

On page 125 the author explains that, after the movie, without any prompting, "my mother began to retell an old story, in a distant voice, as though she were telling it to herself."

"It wasn't your father's fault that he left, you know. I divorced him. When the two of us got married, your grandparents weren't happy with the idea. But they said okay – they probably couldn't have stopped us anyway, and they eventually came around to the idea that it was the right thing to do. Then Barack's father – your grandfather Hussein – wrote Gramps this long nasty letter saying that he didn't approve of the marriage. He didn't want the Obama blood sullied by a white woman, he said. And then there was a problem with your father's first wife. . . he had told me they were separated, but it was a village wedding, so there was no legal document that could show a divorce. . ."

Readers might ponder that passage. If Gramps ever said anything about such a letter, it does not emerge in the narrative. The mother seems to realize the problems. Her chin had begun to tremble, the author writes, and she bit down on her lip, steadying herself.

"Your father wrote back, saying he was going ahead with it. Then you were born, and we agreed that the three of us would return to Kenya after he finished his studies. But your grandfather Hussein was still writing to your father, threatening to have his student visa revoked. By this time Toot had become hysterical – she had read about the Mau-Mau rebellion in Kenya few years earlier, which the Western press really played up – and was sure that I would have my head chopped off and you would be taken away.

"When your father graduated from UH he received two scholarship offers. One was to the New School here in New York. The other was to Harvard. The New School agreed to pay for everything, room and board, a job on the campus, enough to support the three of us. Harvard just agreed to pay tuition. But Barack was such a stubborn bastard, he had to go to Harvard. How can I refuse the best education? he told me. That's all he could think about, proving that he was the best."

"We were so young, you know. I was younger than you are now. He was only a few years older than that. Later, when he came to visit us in Hawaii that time, he wanted us to come live with him. But I was still married to Lolo then, and his third wife had just left him, and I just didn't think . . ."

By now readers recognize that, as Gramps might say, things are pretty complicated with this group. In the Kenyan's visit to Hawaii "that time," none of these details came forth. If the Kenyan, married to his third wife and with a large family, had wanted the author's mother Ann to leave Lolo the Indonesian and move to Kenya, that is something any child would be certain to remember. But maybe the mother knows that is all irretrievably lost, because she has more to say.

"Did I ever tell you that he was late for our first date? He told friends 'you see, gentlemen. I told you that she was a fine girl, and that she would wait for me.'"

The author, meanwhile, was finding the career path that was in his genes.

"The Old Man used to talk about you so much!"

"I decided to become a community organizer," the author explains, on page 133 of *Dreams from My Father*. He saw the need for change, particularly in the White House where "Reagan and his minions were carrying on their dirty deeds." In the style of Gramps, readers might find this of great interest. For one thing, dirty deeds were not in short supply at the time, and the record suggests that the Communists held a strong lead.

During the 1970s in Cambodia, the Khmer Rouge murdered nearly two million people, more than 20 percent of the population, one of the worst cases of genocide in history. See *Murder of a Gentle Land: The Untold Story of a Communist Genocide in Cambodia*, by Anthony Paul and John Barron. The victorious Vietnamese regime, more repressive than its Soviet sponsors, herded people into re-education camps. See *The Vietnamese Gulag* by democracy activist Doan Van Toai. The Soviet Union persecuted dissidents, invaded Afghanistan, and shot down Korean Airlines flight 007 killing 269 people including U.S. congressman Lawrence McDonald. East Germany still walled in its subjects and shot those who attempted to flee. So did the Cuban regime of Fidel Castro, which also persecuted novelists, poets and homosexuals. See the film *Improper Conduct*, by Nestor Almendros.

In *Dreams from My Father*, none of this appears to qualify as dirty deeds and the author avoids it entirely, just as he avoided those liberated after the fall of the USSR. At the time of writing, Islamic terrorism was also on the rise. During the presidency of Jimmy Carter, Iran's Islamist regime, headed by the Ayatollah Khomeini, invaded the U.S. embassy and held 52 Americans hostage for 444 days, from November 4, 1979 to January 20, 1981. In 1989, Khomeini issued a death sentence on author Salman Rushdie, and his publishers, for *The Satanic Verses*. Anyone killing them, the Ayatollah's *fatwa* said, would go directly to heaven.

For the author of *Dreams from My Father*, none of this qualifies as dirty deeds. In this useful fiction, the only villain is Ronald Reagan, and that is no surprise given the author's influences.

Reagan and fellow liberal Democrat and union leader Roy Brewer won strategic victories over a Communist offensive in the movie industry during the late 1940s. A major player in that conflict was longshore boss Harry Bridges, Frank's Communist comrade in Hawaii. Reagan's concept of the Cold War was "we win, they lose." He enraged the left by describing the Soviet Union as an evil empire, which it was. On the other hand, for Frank and the American left, the United States of America was the evil empire.

Reagan described an anti-communist as someone who actually understands Marx and Lenin. He told Gorbachev to "tear down this wall" and fought Soviet proxies in Central America. And when Islamic terrorists killed Americans, he deployed fighter jets to chase them down, proclaiming, "you can run but you can't hide."

The author of *Dreams from My Father* does not specify Reagan's dirty deeds in the White House, or what he planned to do about them. Readers might note, however, that on page 133, the author does provide more detail on his career choice.

"Becoming an organizer was part of a larger narrative, starting with my father and his father before him, my mother and her parents, my memories of Indonesia with its beggars and farmers and the loss of Lolo to power, on through Ray and Frank, Marcus and Regina; my move to New York and my father's death. I can see that my choices were never truly mine alone – and that is how it should be, that to assert otherwise is to chase after a sorry sort of freedom."

Readers will doubtless find this of great interest, for a number of reasons. For one thing, the Kenyan Barack Obama, and his father before him, never did anything that could be described as community organizing. Even so, it's all part of a "larger narrative." It wasn't the author's choice, as he explained when his mother told him that his brains and his character came from his father. So when the author says "I decided to become a community organizer," he means something else, and in this tale that should come as no surprise.

In *Dreams from My Father*, the author has family in Africa but he never appears to consider living there, even on a short-term basis, say, like those in the Peace Corps. His first choice is Chicago, a city he had first visited "the summer after my father's visit to Hawaii, before my eleventh birthday."

The author had told readers that "during his years in Chicago," Frank had enjoyed some modest notoriety as a contemporary of Richard Wright and Langston Hughes. And Frank was not a forgotten man in the Windy City. In the style of Gramps, the reader might believe it was Frank, not the radical black students, who gave the Hawaiian-born community organizer instant credibility. In these circles, it matters very much who your daddy was. The author is not entirely forgetful.

"I imagined Frank in a baggy suit and wide lapels," he writes, "standing in front of the old Regal Theatre, waiting to see Duke or Ella emerge from a gig."

Being a community organizer was "part of the larger narrative" through Frank, among others. The author says he also received a call from someone he calls Marty Kaufmann, "a white man of medium height wearing a rumpled suit over a pudgy frame. His face was heavy with two-day-old whiskers: behind a pair of thick, wire-rimmed glasses, his eyes set in a perpetual squint."

Marty asks why somebody from Hawaii wants to be an organizer, says he must be angry about something, and stresses that anger is a requirement for the job. Marty was "Jewish, in his late thirties, had been reared in New York. He had started organizing in the sixties with the student protests, and ended up staying with it for fifteen years. Farmers in Nebraska, Blacks in Philadelphia. Mexicans in Chicago." Marty needed somebody black to work in the churches, and offered the newcomer ten thousand dollars the first year, with a two thousand dollar travel allowance. Still, the prospect says, "there was something about him that made me wary." Marty was a little too sure of himself, "and white – he'd said himself that was a problem."

The eager organizer also hangs out with Rafiq Al Shabaz, who tells him, "If it hadn't been for Islam, man, I'd probably be dead."

The author gets no further contact with Aunt Jane, who in 1982 called from Nairobi to tell Barry his father had passed away, and that he should break the news to his unnamed uncle in Boston. At no point in the narrative does the Hawaiian-born American get any information on the Kenyan from any uncle in Boston. One day, however, his sister Auma duly arrives from Africa, full of information on the Kenyan.

"The Old Man," says the author on page 208, "That's what Auma called our father, and it was familiar and distant, an elemental force that isn't fully understood." She held up the picture of their father "that sat on my bookshelf, a studio portrait that my mother had saved." Auma held it to his face and said "you have the same mouth."

The studio portrait Auma was holding did not find its way into *Dreams from My Father*. The author is telling readers to accept sister Auma's word that the Kenyan Old Man and his American son have the same mouth. In the style of Gramps, readers who compare the photos might not think so.

At one point the author asks Auma to tell what she remembers about the Old Man.

"I can't say I really knew him, Barack. Maybe nobody did. . . not really. His life was so scattered. People only knew scraps and pieces, even his own children."

Readers might note that, unlike Aunt Jane, who used "Barry," Auma uses "Barack" for the American and "Old Man" for the Kenyan. Of course, the author already explained that the Kenyan "bequeathed" his name to him, so no surprise that, in this account, Auma fails to use it for the rightful owner. If they weren't convinced already, readers might think the Old Man has a real identity problem. Maybe nobody knew him. But Auma reveals a key detail.

"He was already away when I was born. In Hawaii with your mum, and then at Harvard."

So when the Kenyan Barack Obama came to Hawaii, he was already married with a family including Auma. This reality meant that any marriage to Ann Dunham would be invalid, and that posed problems for the prospect of an official divorce. The eager Auma does not trouble herself with the details.

When he came back to Kenya, she explains, "I was too young to remember much about him coming." But he had an American wife named Ruth, "the first white person I had been near."

The Old Man was "working for an American oil company – Shell, I think." And the Old Man was "well connected with all the top government people." In fact, as Auma explains, "the Old Man, he left the American company to work in the government, for the Ministry of Tourism."

These jobs would be a matter of record, especially the government post. At any point in his career, those positions would have would have been quite a talking point for the man's American-born son, but he appears to have made no effort whatsoever to gather the information. Or maybe he did, and then it was irretrievably lost, like the memories of the month-long visit in Hawaii. In this narrative, he has to get the story hearsay from Auma, who early in the conversion said she didn't really know the Old Man, and maybe nobody did.

Auma never describes the Old Man as a pro-Soviet Marxist. In her account, the Kenyan's big issue is tribalism, which he claimed would ruin the country. He always thought he knew best, Auma said, and "When he was passed up for a promotion he complained loudly. 'How can you be my senior,' he would say to one of the ministers, 'and yet I am teaching you how to do your job properly.' Word got back to Kenyatta that the Old Man was a troublemaker."

Thus, Auma, the woman who didn't really know the Old Man, can rattle off quotes of what he said in the workplace, and she knew all about the intrigues in the Kenyan government, headed by strongman Jomo Kenyatta.

The Old Man fell on hard times, Auma said, and had to borrow money for food. "He would stagger in drunk and come into my room." After Kenyatta died, the Old Man's situation improved. "He got a job with the Ministry of Finance and started to have money again, and influence." Still, he was bitter at "seeing his other age-mates who had been more politically astute rise ahead of him. And it was too late to pick up the pieces of his family." For a long time, Auma said, he lived alone in a hotel room.

"I almost never saw him," she said. "We were like strangers."

Readers might recall the biblical epigraph from 1 Chronicles 29:15: "For we are strangers before them, and sojourners, as were all our fathers."

Later as she stared at "our father's photograph," Auma laments between sobs, "I was just starting to know him." So when he died, "I felt so cheated. As cheated as you must have felt." But Auma has good news too.

"You know, the Old Man used to talk about you so much! He would show off your picture to everybody and tell us how well you were doing in school."

Auma, alas, doesn't have the picture the Old Man showed off to everybody. But then, she didn't really know him, and maybe nobody did, though she remembers his American wife Ruth, the first white person she had been near. He was like a stranger, after all. And as readers might have noticed, Auma provides no information on the Old Man's brother, the author's uncle in Boston mentioned by Aunt Jane in her 1982 telephone call. All told, this quite a performance and readers might check what presidential biographers, PBS documentarians, and establishment journalists said about it, particularly the transformation of the Kenyan Barack H. Obama into a nameless "Old Man." As Gramps might say, this dramatic narrative requires constant suspension of disbelief.

After the session with Auma, the son says, "All my life I had carried a single image of my father." That stands at odds with his earlier statements that he preferred the father's more distant image, "an image I could alter on a whim or ignore when convenient." Now it's a single image (page 220), "one that I had sometimes rebelled against but had never questioned, one that I had later tried to take as my own. The brilliant scholar, the generous friend, the upstanding leader – my father had been all those things."

The author goes on to tout the black men he knew, "Frank or Ray or Will or Rafiq." Readers might note that Frank's name comes first and that the Kenyan Barack Obama, also known as the Old Man, does not even make the list. These men might have fallen short of the standards of "Martin and Malcolm, DuBois and Mandela," but "I had learned to respect these men for the struggles they went through, recognizing them as my own."

Readers may notice that *Dreams from My Father* contains little about The Rev. Martin Luther King Jr., and that is not accidental. The black Stalinists like Frank hated King and derided him as "De Lawd," the divine character from *The Green Pastures*. American Communists preached Lenin's belief that all worship of a divinity was necrophilia, and non-violent resistance was not part of their platform.

Barack, meanwhile, is now in a position to hire people. One employee, Johnnie, asks "Why haven't you ever gone to Kenya?"

"I don't know. Maybe I'm scared of what I'll find out."

Note that Johnnie does not ask the author what, exactly, he might find in Kenya that would scare him. Johnnie helps him work with various churchmen, including the Reverend Jeremiah Wright, Jr. (page 274), "a dynamic young pastor. His message seemed to appeal to young people like me."

Wright was a former member of the Nation of Islam but his church had shed little, if anything, of the racist gospel. The author's spiritual guide, as Barry Rubin observes, was "a man who is radical, anti-American, and anti-Semitic and who openly confessed his hatred of whites and Jews." For his part, the author is uncritical of the dynamic young pastor.

The Rev. Wright tells him "life's not safe for a black man in this country, Barack. Never has been. Probably never will be." Yet, he titles a sermon "the audacity of hope." In these quarters, Barack ruminates:

"The relationship between black and white, the meaning of escape, would never be quite the same for me as it had been for Frank or for the Old Man."

Note that here the author puts the two men in the same sentence and Frank again takes priority. But in this useful fiction, the Old Man is not about to disappear. Obama Jr. is soon off to Kenya, now evidently unafraid of what he will find there.

In *Dreams from My Father* dates are scarce as the Old Man, but the author makes it clear this is his first trip to Kenya. If the Kenyan Old Man was indeed his father, readers might think, the son would have made many more trips, especially when his father was alive. He would be eager to visit the man of unsurpassed concentration, who graduated in three years, served as the first president of the International Students Association, and went on to Harvard.

By all indications, the author did not attend the funeral of the man he says is his father, with whom his mother had supposedly stayed in touch, even though married to the Indonesian Lolo Soetoro. By some accounts, the author did attend the funeral of Frank Marshall Davis in 1987, but readers will not find that reality in *Dreams from My Father*. By the time he makes the first trip to Kenya, the Old Man is dead but his fame lives on.

"You wouldn't be related to Dr. Obama by any chance?" asks Miss Omoro, a woman at the airport.

"Well, yes," he says. "He was my father."

"I'm very sorry about his passing," Miss Omoro says. "Your father was a close friend of my family's. He would often come to our house as a child."

It is an exchange of great significance.

"She'd recognized my name," the author explains. "That had never happened before. . . for the first time in my life, I felt the comfort, the firmness of identity that a name might provide."

The bequeathing of the name Barack Obama to the Hawaiian-born American may not abound in official documentation, but as far as the author is concerned, it's now a done deal. The narrative is all coming together for him and he's feeling good about himself, with "the comfort, the firmness of identity that a name might provide."

He soon hooks up with Auma, and Auntie Zeituni, "our father's sister."

Here in Kenya, the author gives "father" a good workout.

"I feel my father's presence as Auma and I walk through the busy street. I see him in the schoolboys who run past us. . . I hear him in the laughter of the pair of university students, . . I smell him in the cigarette smoke of the businessman... in the sweat of the day laborer." Indeed, "the Old Man's here, I think, although he doesn't say anything to me. He's here, asking me to understand."

Toward the end of his second week in Kenya, he and Auma go on a safari. "Like most Kenyans," the author says, "she could draw a straight line between game parks and colonialism." Like "father," colonialism is a prevalent theme. The author is asking the reader to understand.

On the lengthy trip he also learns about his grandfather, Onyango, who had converted to Islam. "Granny" is still around, and tells him many stories about Onyango and his son Barack. Granny explains that she and Onyango received "a letter from Barack saying he had met this American girl, Ann, and that he would like to marry her." Onyango reportedly objected because of Barack's responsibilities at home and doubts whether Ann would come to Kenya and live as a Luo. The letter itself does not appear in *Dreams from My Father*, but Barack Jr. asks Granny if she has anything left of the Old Man or Onyango. She rummages through an old leather trunk and brings forth a document.

Domestic Servant's Pocket Register, reads the cover, and under in smaller letters, *Issued under the Authority of the Registration of Domestic Servant's Ordinance, 1928, Colony and Protectorate of Kenya*. The inside cover bears Onyango's left and right thumbprints. The box was empty where the photograph had been.

The document provides the Native Registration Ordinance No. Rsl A NBI 0976717. The preamble explains: "The object of this Ordinance is to provide every person employed in a domestic capacity with a record of such employment and to safeguard his or her interests as well as to protect employers against the employment of persons who have rendered themselves unsuitable for such work." Servant is defined as: cook, house servant, waiter, butler, nurse, valet, bar boy, footmen or chauffeur, or washerman. Those found working without passbooks are "liable to fine no exceeding one hundred shillings or imprisonment not exceeding six months or to both."

This passbook is for Hussein II Onyango:

Race or tribe. Ja'Luo
Complexion: dark
Nose: flat
Mouth: large
Hair: Curly
Teeth: Six missing

The passbook includes some complimentary notes from employers. But Mr. Arthur W. H. Cole of East Africa Survey Group says he found Onyango unsuitable for the job and not worth 60 shillings a month. In the style of the *Honolulu Star-Bulletin* article, the birth certificate, and the vaccination records, *Dreams from my Father* includes no photo of this document. The author's account of it is peculiar. The *Official Gazette of the Colony and Protectorate of Kenya*, April 12, 1922, gives the Native Registration Ordinance of 1921 as number S. 9392/17. It mentions a Certificate of Identification but not a passbook. If the certificate is lost, the fee for replacement is two shillings. Passbooks were characteristic of South Africa under the apartheid regime, which the author may have been trying to evoke in his version of *Roots*.

Back home, Obama gets engaged and takes Michelle to Kenya.

"She was an immediate success there," the author says, "in part because the number of Luo words in her vocabulary very soon surpassed mine."

The author provides no examples of Luo words that he and Michelle knew. He does not indicate that the Luo people speak Dholuo, Swahili, and English. Meanwhile, the audacious, hopeful Rev. Wright marries them, with family in attendance.

"The person who made me proudest of all was Roy," the author says. "Actually, now we call him Abongo, his Luo name, for two years ago he decided to reassert his African heritage. He converted to Islam and had sworn off pork and tobacco and alcohol." Roy, his African brother, also pronounces (page 441) on "the need for the black man to liberate himself from the poisoning influences of European culture, and he scolds aunt Auma for her European ways."

Note how the author links African heritage to Islam, even though Africa is a continent of great religious diversity, with Christianity accounting for some 40 percent of the population. Maybe the author knew that, but had forgotten it, in the style of the Kenyan's Hawaiian visit.

All told, this is quite a tale, and readers might give it careful thought. Political biographies abound and, ghost-written or otherwise, generally take pains to portray their subject in the best possible light and ignore or downplay potential embarrassments. *Dreams from My Father* is a far more ambitious project. As Gramps might say, it's like a bikini: what it reveals is interesting but what it conceals is crucial.

"A black man from Kansas named Frank."

The author, who has a stubborn desire to protect himself from scrutiny, is out to make a name for himself, but not in the usual way through proven accomplishment. Instead he rips off the name from the Kenyan, just as Hannibal Lecter peeled the face off a dead cop in *Silence of the Lambs*. The Kenyan then becomes simply a nameless "Old Man," in effect, a non-person.

After the collapse of Communism, the author knows he's not going anywhere politically if the truth about Frank Marshall Davis comes out. So he camouflages the high-profile Stalinist as Frank, the Grady Wilson-like happy drunk, warning about the dangers of womenfolk. By the time the book emerges, Frank, the Kenyan, Gramps, Lolo, Ann Dunham and Mabel Hefty are all dead, unable to render reviews, favorable or otherwise. The narrative is also highly didactic, and at pains to create symmetry between British colonialism in Kenya and America as a settler-colonial state based on oppression, exploitation and racism. It's a tall order, but the author tips his hand with the "myth," "tales" and the "useful fiction." He can't honestly say that the voice in the book is not his, a confession that a ventriloquist is at work, but if people have trouble taking him at face value, he doesn't fault their suspicions. In the style of Gramps, readers might have a hard time finding that "granite slab of truth."

Beyond the confessional aspect, the book is highly contradictory in what it affirms. As prosecutors know, it's harder for someone to keep straight stories that have no basis in fact. The tale is bulked with evasive filler, the elephantine style blurring the contours like a coating of mud. The fact-checker had an existential problem. Little if any documentation, few dates, no photo section, no photo credits, and squads of characters given first names only, including Frank. So it can hardly be an accident that *Dreams from My Father* fails to include an index. The fakery leapt off the pages but nobody seemed to notice.

"Perceptive and wise," says the front cover endorsement from Marian Wright Edelman, "this book will tell you something about yourself whether you are black or white."

"Beautifully crafted. . . moving and candid," says novelist Scott Turow on the back cover. "This book belongs on the shelf beside works like James McBride's *The Color of Water* and Gregory Howard Williams's *Life on the Color Line* as a tale of living astride America's racial categories."

"Provocative," wrote the *New York Times Book Review*. "Persuasively describes the phenomenon of belonging to two different worlds, and thus belonging to neither."

Turning to the other national newspaper of record, the *Washington Post Book World* said, "Fluidly, calmly insightful, Obama guides us straight to the intersection of the most serious questions of identity, class and race."

For Alex Kadowitz author of *There are no Children Here*. "Obama's writing is incisive yet forgiving. This is a book worth savoring."

"One of the most powerful books of self-discovery I've ever read," opined Charlayne Hunter-Gault, author of *In My Place* and PBS correspondent. "It is also beautifully written, skillfully layered, and paced like a novel."

This response reflects the prevailing establishment view that a narrative need not be factually correct to be politically correct. The critics, in effect, had all become Roger Ebert, responding with a thumbs up, the only other alternative being thumbs down. The politically correct critical school has no use for nuance or detail. As another event showed, critical faculties seem to have been suspended.

Shortly after the initial release of *Dreams from My Father* in 1995, the author appeared on the "Connie Martinson Talks Books" show on public television, which debuted in 1979. Martinson is a member of the National Book Critics Circle and in the early going it was clear she had actually read the book. She noted that her guest had gone to Occidental College in Los Angeles but wound up in Chicago through "Marty."

"I call him Marty," her guest said, momentarily uncomfortable. "That's a pseudonym."

Such an admission on a television show might prompt a veteran of the National Book Critics Circle, who had interviewed authors such as Studs Terkel, Gore Vidal, and Vincent Bugliosi, to tender a question such as "Who is the real person?" or "Why did you use a pseudonym? Isn't this a non-fiction book?" Or, "Why the need to hide Marty Kauffman's true identity?"

The most likely candidate for Marty is Jerry Kellman, a protégé of *Rules for Radicals* author Saul Alinsky, who combined leftist ideology with Mafia tactics.

Connie Martinson, who had taught at UCLA, did no such thing. She failed to kindle and listened in rapture as her guest told the television audience he became a community organizer, "to reestablish the dreams and idealism that brought my parents together." Then she asked him to read from *Dreams from My Father*, which he did. So it wasn't so much an interview as a recital, like something from Oprah Winfrey's show. So was a September 20, 1995 speech the author gave at the Cambridge public library, which aired on Channel 37 Cambridge Municipal Television as part of "The Author Series."

"My father was a black African," he said. "My mother a white American" and "as mid-American as you could get." He is "trying to make sense of my family" and explains that "my father's family came from a small Kenyan village" and his grandfather was one of first to see and have contact with a white person.

The African father and American mother met in Hawaii, "swept up in idealism," and a sense of "community, equity and fairness." But their marriage broke apart. The author reads a passage from the book in which he is angry because his father is absent. He laments that he is "without father figures around me."

The author could have read from the Kenyan's essay "Problems of Our Socialism," in the July 1965 issue of *East Africa Journal*. There the Kenyan, a man of the left, discussed taxes and outlined his preference for statist-style government, while rejecting old-style Marxism and Communism. Instead of citing anything from the Kenyan, he introduces "a black man from Kansas named Frank." He was a "fairly well known poet, moved to Hawaii and lived there." This poet was "Frank Marshall Davis," the speaker said, and "a close friend of my maternal grandfather."

Then about nine minutes into the presentation, he reads a long passage from the book, beginning on page 85, going through his reading of Baldwin, DuBois, Ellison et al, and Malcolm X, and his wish that his white blood might be expunged. The reading includes the lament that Malcolm "don't talk about no pussy" and Ray proclaiming that he needs no book telling him how to be black. The reading winds up at Frank's place in Waikiki, and the speaker gives Frank a hip accent rather unlike his actual voice. Frank ruminates about blacks and whites and he agrees that the speaker's grandmother is right.

"She understands that black people have a reason to hate. That's how it is. For your sake, I wish it were otherwise, but it's not so. So you might as well get used to it."

So the jovial Frank is out to justify hatred, and readers might give that some thought. Frank is the central character in this passage, but the speaker gets the curtain line.

"The earth shook under my feet, ready to crack open at any moment. I stopped, trying to steady myself, and knew for the first time that I was utterly alone." That ends the long reading, and applause rings out.

By openly identifying Frank Marshall Davis on a television program, the speaker was handing critics the keys to the mystery, but investigative reporters did not appear eager to follow up. Likewise, the true identities of the pseudonyms and first-name-only characters remained unexplored. Who was "Marty" anyway? A Kenyan visits his American son for a month, and the kid has no memory of it? Wasn't he already married, with a family, when he came to Hawaii? Why no dates and bylines for the newspaper article? Who is the African woman in the cover photo? How can an African woman barely know the Old Man, yet rattle on about him at length? What does it mean that the Kenyan is a prop in someone else's narrative? And what's all this about a useful fiction?

As they say the questions go on and on, but to get an answer one has to ask. Those purporting to be critics, pundits, and literati declined to do so. He had mentioned Richard Wright, but nobody seemed eager to ask the author what he thought of Wright's contribution to *The God That Failed*. African-American authors such as Chester Himes, author of *Lonely Crusade*, seemed to have escaped his notice, along with the landmark books of recent times. For example, the author shows no sign that he had read *The Road To Serfdom* by F.A. Hayek, a book fully endorsed by John Maynard Keynes, or *The Gulag Archipelago*, by Alexander Solzhenitsyn, the Nobel laureate. Readers might recall that President Ford and Secretary of State Henry Kissinger, had declined to meet with the great Russian writer, who discovered that "the line separating good and evil passes not through states, nor between classes, nor between political parties either – but right through every human heart – and through all human hearts."

For their part, the author and his narrator were glad they had not cut the 50 pages. They would not tell the story differently in 2004 "even if certain passages have proven to be inconvenient politically, the grist for pundit commentary and opposition research." The narrator thus concedes that this entire enterprise is ad copy, promotional material for a politician on the rise. But he still has that strong desire to protect himself from scrutiny, with good reason.

"My father was an African American, born and raised in Kansas, and college educated. He loved jazz, wrote poetry and made a name for himself in Chicago. A prolific journalist interested in politics, he chose to join the Communist Party, dominated by whites. He spent most of his life as a propagandist for the Soviet Union, ruled by an all-white dictatorship. They made some mistakes but, more important, they wanted a better world. My father wanted a better world, and so do I."

Such an introduction would have suited the man the author lovingly described as "Pop," but even the Democratic Party is unlikely to welcome Pop the Stalinist with open arms. The author knows he's going nowhere if the truth about Frank comes out, and here readers might consider another issue.

More than a few Americans grew up with Communist parents,

Radical Son author David Horowitz for example, but came to reject that totalitarian ideology and speak out against it. Had the author of *Dreams from My Father* rejected Frank's orthodox Communism, and spoken out against the USSR, that would have gained him broader support and respect. The trouble is, by all indications, the author accepted Frank's orthodoxies and remained uncritical of the Soviet Union, even after it fell. That is why he needs a different narrative, something more along these lines:

"My father was a foreign student, born and raised in a small village in Kenya. He grew up herding goats, went to school in a tin-roof shack. His father, my grandfather, was a cook, a domestic servant to the British."

That was the candidate calling himself Barack Obama in his keynote address to the Democratic Party convention on July, 27, 2004. The 2004 edition of *Dreams from My Father* included the entire speech and that year the author won his race for U.S. Senator from Illinois, defeating Alan Keyes, also an African American, by a wide margin. In 2005 an audio version of the *Dreams* book appeared with a significant omission: every trace of Frank had been removed. So Frank was the reason the author's stubborn desire to protect himself remained strong. In politics, as the Kennedy and Bush families know, it does matter who your daddy was.

That year the U.S. Senator for Illinois won a Grammy for the audio version, bagging the prize for best spoken word over Garrison Keillor's *The Adventures of Guy Noir: Radio Private Eye*, *The Al Franken Show Party*, Bob Dylan's *Chronicles: Volume One*, and *When Will Jesus Bring the Pork Chops?* by George Carlin. But the rising star did not rest on his laurels. With his new identity, and the uncritical reception of *Dreams from My Father*, the possibilities seemed endless.

"I am a prisoner of my own biography."

The Audacity of Hope: Thoughts on Reclaiming the American Dream appeared in 2006 and readers could see the difference right up front. The Hawaiian-born American calling himself Barack Obama is on the cover, which shows no thatched huts or any African motif. To judge by the imagery, the dreams from his father have been replaced by the American dream, or so it seems. The book bears no biblical epigraph about strangers.

"To the women who raised me," the dedication reads, "my Maternal Grandmother, Tutu, who has been a rock of stability throughout my life, and my mother, whose loving spirit sustains me still."

The author with all those dreams from his father is pretty much a momma's boy now. Still, people ask, "where'd you get that funny name?" On page 10, he explains:

"I am a prisoner of my own biography: I can't help but view the American experience through the lens of a black man of mixed heritage, forever mindful of how generations of people who looked like me were subjugated and stigmatized, and the subtle and not so subtle ways that race and class continue to shape our lives."

The key phrase is "prisoner of my own biography," the story of the African father from Kenya and the American mother from Kansas. That's the story in *Dreams from My Father* and the author realizes there's no escape from it. That's what happens once you put it out there, and the biography finds widespread acceptance in establishment circles. On the other hand, the Kenyan Old Man plays little role in *The Audacity of Hope*, where the mother is the prime mover.

"Much of what I absorbed from the sixties was filtered through my mother," the author explains, "who to the end of her life would proudly proclaim herself an unreconstructed liberal. The civil rights movement in particular inspired her reverence; whenever the opportunity presented itself, she would drill into me the values that she saw there: tolerance, equality, standing up for the disadvantaged." His mother, "worked mightily to instill in me the values that many Americans learn in Sunday school; honesty, empathy, discipline, delayed gratification, and hard work. She raged at poverty and injustice and scorned those who were indifferent to both."

She did this without the help of religious texts or outside authorities, but she did teach him about religion. This differs from the account in *Dreams from My Father*, in which the mother refuses to describe her faith as religious and even finds it "sacrilegious." And she was a "lonely witness for secular humanism." Readers might note how *The Audacity of Hope* transforms Ann Dunham into a veritable one-woman ecumenical movement.

"In her mind," the author says, "a working knowledge of the world's great religions was a necessary part of any well-rounded education. In our household, the Bible, the Koran, and the Bhagavad Gita sat on the shelf alongside books of Greek and Norse and African mythology." The author does not single out any book as particularly influential, as he did *The Autobiography of Malcolm X* in *Dreams from My Father*.

The *Audacity of Hope* does not recall Malik, the Nation of Islam convert who explained that Malcolm X "tells it like it is, no doubt about it," even though Malcolm, as another character said, "don't talk about no pussy."

The author includes nothing about the Nation of Islam belief that the author's mother Ann Dunham, like Hillary Clinton, Eleanor Roosevelt and Jane Fonda, is the result of Yakub's experiment on the Isle of Patmos more than 6,000 years ago. The author is not a theologian and shows no familiarity with landmark books on religion and politics such as *The Naked Public Square*, by Richard John Neuhaus, a colleague of Martin Luther King in the anti-war and civil-rights movements. On the other hand, the author seems to show a flair for political philosophy.

He quotes the Declaration of Independence and traces its roots to eighteenth-century liberal and republican thought. The value of individual freedom, he writes, was "as radical as Martin Luther's posting on the church door." Much of humanity finds scant evidence of freedom in their lives.

"In fact," the author explains, "my appreciation of the Bill of Rights comes from having spent part of my childhood in Indonesia and from still having family in Kenya, countries where individual rights are almost entirely subject to the self-restraint of army generals or the whims of corrupt bureaucrats."

So mom is now more central than the Kenyan, but note that Kenya is still in play, here as an example of bad government. The author's description would seem to fit Indonesia more than Kenya, for all its difficulties one of the more democratic countries in Africa. The most repressive African regime of modern times was not Kenya or South Africa but Ethiopia under the Marxist-Leninist regime of Col. Mengistu Haile Mariam. Even as a British colony, freedom, democracy and human rights thrived more in Kenya than Tanzania and Mozambique, whose flag bears the image of a Russian AK-47 assault rifle. As in *Dreams*, those regimes escape notice here.

The author says he took Michelle to Kenya shortly before they were married and "we had a wonderful time, visiting my grandmother up-country." Where, exactly "up-country" might be on the map is not noted, but the folksy formulation seems to indicate a certain familiarity with the nation of Kenya. On the flight back to Chicago, Michelle says "I never realized just how American I was."

If the author experiences any feelings like Michelle's he keeps them to himself. In *Dreams from My Father*, his role models are his Kenyan father and grandfather. In *The Audacity of Hope* he draws lessons from Paul Simon, the white U.S. Senator from Illinois, admiring his honesty, character, and sense of empathy. And "like most of my values, I learned about empathy from my mother. She disdained any kind of cruelty or thoughtlessness or abuse of power." On this theme, the author cites an additional source.

"But it was my relationship with my grandfather that I think I first internalized the full meaning of empathy," and this is not the Kenyan Hussein II Onyango, who worked as a servant to the British. The author is talking about old Gramps his own self, Stanley Dunham, the white American from the Kansas heartland who might have thought that the Kenyan looked like Nat King Cole.

"I often lived with my grandparents during my high school years, and without a father present in the house, my grandfather bore the brunt of much of my adolescent rebellion." As for the Kenyan:

"My father was almost entirely absent from my childhood, having been divorced from my mother when I was two years told." But on page 204 the reader gets some insights on the man.

"Although my father had been raised a Muslim, by the time he met my mother he was a confirmed atheist, thinking religion to be so much superstition, like the mumbo-jumbo of witch doctors that he had witnessed in the Kenyan villages of his youth."

In *Dreams from My Father,* the mother explained that the Kenyan had lived his life according to principles that promised "a higher form of power." Since religion is just so much superstition and mumbo-jumbo to the atheistic Kenyan, those principles are probably political, not spiritual.

Maybe the Kenyan had explained all that during the month-long visit, and it was all coming back to the author now. So it wasn't irretrievably lost after all. In *Dreams from My Father*, Hussein Onyango Obama had been a prominent farmer, tribal elder and "a medicine man with healing powers." Note the transition from "medicine man" to "witch doctors" and such.

Readers might recall that the author preferred his father's more distant image, which he could "alter on a whim or ignore when convenient." As it happens, Frank was a confirmed atheist who believed religion to be so much superstition and mumbo-jumbo. In this account, the author attributes all that to the Kenyan, just as he altered the Kenyan into a jazz enthusiast. As for his own upbringing, religion definitely plays a role.

During the five years the author lived with his stepfather Lolo Soetoro in Indonesia, he writes (page 204), "I was first sent to a neighborhood Catholic school, and then to a predominantly Muslim school."

Catholicism has not been a theme of this narrative, and the author's mother is something of a secularist. Readers are not told who "sent" the author to the neighborhood Catholic school, here unnamed but by some accounts Santo Fransiskus Asisis, where according to the *Washington Post* the student was "registered as a Muslim," the religion of his stepfather. From there it was on to the "predominantly Muslim school," also unnamed but by some accounts Besuki, run by the Indonesian government, complete with a mosque. Readers will have a hard time looking into this school because the registration records were supposedly destroyed by flooding. It has emerged, however, that the author received instruction in Islam.

Based on *The Audacity of Hope*, readers might feel free to call the president "predominantly Muslim," like his school. Maybe some other Muslim students practiced Christianity, Buddhism or Judaism on a part-time basis. And the non-Muslim students, if any – remember the records were destroyed by flooding – perhaps practiced Islam on certain days of the week.

The author does not indicate whether, like the Kenyan, he ever believed that the Muslim and Catholic faiths were so much superstition, like the mumbo-jumbo of witch doctors. Or as the Kenyan Old Man might have believed, was Islam or the Nation of Islam only so much superstition and mumbo-jumbo? Readers will find no word on that in *The Audacity of Hope*, but in both the Catholic and predominantly Muslim schools his mother's main concern was "with whether I was properly learning my multiplication tables."

Though the book downplays the Kenyan Barack Obama, the author takes care to remind the reader that he is a "prisoner" of his own biography. His unnamed "cousin in Kenya," for example, complains that it is impossible to find work unless he pays a bribe.

The *Audacity of Hope* title, readers learn, comes from a sermon by the Rev. Jeremiah Wright, whose anti-American fulminations, "god damn America," that sort of thing, get no coverage here. The book is packed with policy wonkery and populist pieties, wrapped in flag-waving patriotism all the way to the last line:

"My heart is filled with love for this country."

Even though, as Frank taught him, equal opportunity and the

American way was "all that shit," the author's heart is filled with love for this country. The critics loved it.

The author was "that rare politician who can actually write," wrote Michiko Kakutani in the *New York Times*, citing the book's "simple common sense," and "level-headed non-partisan prose."

John Balzer of the *Los Angeles Times* praised the author's "fresh and buoyant vocabulary to scrub away some of the toxins from contemporary political debate."

For Michael Kazin of the *Washington Post*, the book's "uplifting, elegant prose does fill one with hope."

And so on, but readers might check to see if the critics missed a few things.

Like *Dreams from My Father* this book lacks a photo section, a significant omission for a book promoting a politician. So the author's need to protect himself from scrutiny is still in play, and he still does not trust readers to believe their own eyes.

The book does boast an index but, alas, it does not include an entry for anyone named Davis, not even Miles Davis. At the Cambridge Library in 1995, the author identified "Frank," as Frank Marshall Davis and in the *Dreams* book Frank gets first place on the author's list of influential black men in his life. If the truth about Frank is known, the author with the stubborn desired to avoid scrutiny knows, he is going nowhere. So no surprise that, in *The Audacity of Hope*, Frank is missing altogether, just as he was from the audio version of *Dreams from My Father*. On the other hand, a key character missing from that book duly shows up in this one.

David Axelrod makes several appearances in *The Audacity of Hope* as a "media consultant," with little background information. In the acknowledgements section, Axelrod heads the list of "good friends" who provided invaluable suggestions. The thirteen others include Anthony Lake, Susan Rice, Cass Sunstein, and Jim Wallis, a key figure on the religious left and founder of *Sojourners* magazine. In 1979, Wallis wrote that the Vietnamese boat people had been inoculated with a taste for Western lifestyle during the war and were "fleeing to support their consumer habit in other lands." Apparently the totalitarian Soviet-backed regime had nothing to do with their flight.

On April 1, 2007, Ben Wallace-Wells profiled David Axelrod in a *New York Times* article headlined, "Obama's Narrator." In this article of more than 5,000 words, the narrator tells Wallace-Wells that Obama is a "trailblazing" figure who "represents the future."

Like Gramps, readers might get the distinct feeling that David Axelrod is really behind this guy. Like Lincoln Steffens, Axelrod has seen the future and it works, but he's not there yet. "So far Obama's campaign has been steeped in his biography," says Wallace-Wells. "This is, after all, a 45-year-old man who has written not one but two memoirs." Wallace-Wells does not get into the authorship question, those doubts about the voice in book, and references to "someone else's narrative." Neither does the journalist indulge any analysis of the two memoirs or ask Obama's narrator who, exactly, Frank might have been, and why Frank had been cut out of the second memoir and the audio version of the first.

Wallace-Wells does note that Axelrod was a former lead political reporter for the *Chicago Tribune* but left that post to work as a political operative. In 1987, *Chicago Magazine* profiled him in "Hatchet Man: The Rise of David Axelrod." Wallace-Wells notes that in the last four years, "Axelrod has helped steer campaigns for fully four of the Democrats now running for president – Obama, Clinton, John Edwards and Chris Dodd." This man specializes in presidential candidates.

So the author of *Dreams from My Father* and *The Audacity of Hope* has good reason to thank the man profiled as "Obama's narrator," who tells reporters that his candidate represents the future itself. The author also thanks Madhuri Kommareddi, who devoted the entire summer before she entered Yale Law School, to "fact-check the entire manuscript" with help from Hillary Schrenell. By all indications, over an entire summer this team found no issues of fact with the biography of which the author was a prisoner. So the fact checkers found true that the Kenyan Barack Obama, though "raised a Muslim" as the author explains, was an atheist who dismissed religion "like the mumbo-jumbo of witch doctors that he had witnessed in the Kenyan villages of his youth."

The checkers did not have to chase down all the facts on Frank because Frank wasn't in the book. As Gramps might say, out of sight, out of mind. And as far as the checkers are concerned, the narrative of the African father and American mother is part of a body of unassailable fact. As it happens, fact-checker Madhuri Kommareddi went on to work as a policy aide on the Obama for America 2008 presidential campaign. Again the candidate would catch some big breaks. The journalistic *zeitgeist* was on his side.

"We are five days away."

Journalists once sought to uncover stories those in power want hidden, such as the Pentagon Papers, the Iran-Contra scandal, CIA misconduct, and so on. With the *Dreams from My Father* candidate, on the other hand, journalists helped cover up what the authors wanted hidden.

Hugh Gregory Gallagher described the dynamic in *FDR's Splendid Deception: The moving story of Roosevelt's massive disability – and the intense efforts to conceal it from the public.* The splendid deception, Gallagher writes, "required substantial physical effort, ingenuity, and bravado," along with collaboration from the press. News stories seldom if ever mentioned FDR's disability and as biographer John Gunther observed, the reality that he used a wheelchair was never printed at all. When FDR fell during a 1932 campaign, reporters failed to mention it. Photographers saw the fall but no photographs were published.

Gallagher's book came out in 1985, so it took 40 years, nearly half a century, for the first serious revelations of FDR's splendid deception. Faking an identity is a more serious matter than concealing a disability. Such a deception also requires effort, ingenuity and bravado, or as one could say, audacity. It also requires the kind of collaboration Julien Benda described as *La Trahison des Clercs*, or, as Roger Kimball titled a 2006 edition, *The Treason of the Intellectuals*.

An obvious hack job like *Dreams from My Father* was a soft underhand lob right down the middle of the plate. Critics should have knocked it out of the park but either failed to take a swing or whiffed entirely. Investigative reporters could have turned the light on the 1995 and 2004 versions, and asked the candidate about Frank Marshall Davis, whom the author had mentioned on television. Material on the old Stalinist was hardly in short supply. His *Livin' the Blues* memoir, though not a big seller, was in libraries everywhere. Why did Frank get lots of ink in 1995 and 2004, then disappear in the 2005 audio book? Why was Frank missing entirely in *The Audacity of Hope*? Who was the real guy behind "Marty" the pseudonym the author used in the television interview? And why the need to use fake names? That guy "Pop" in the poem at Occidental, who was he, anyway? As they say, nobody popped the questions. Some mysterious El Niño had infantilized the media, which wasn't what it used to be in regards to the truth.

Shortly before the 1993 Super Bowl NBC aired an announcement that violence against women surged 40 percent on Super Bowl Sunday. The announcement cited "studies" that on the day of the Big Game crazed husbands and boyfriends went wild and beat the hell out of their wives and girlfriends. The *Boston Globe*, *New York Times* and other major newspapers echoed the claims uncritically. In the entire nation only a single reporter, Ken Ringle of the *Washington Post*, bothered to check the sources to see if the story was true, which it wasn't. But Ringle was not praised for exposing the hoax. Indeed, the intrepid reporter soon found himself under attack for exploding the hoax, and fakery was becoming a trend.

Jayson Blair of the *New York Times* faked numerous stories but by the time his bosses took action he had ascended from intern to the national desk. Stephen Glass faked many stories at *The New Republic* but endured for three years before being fired in 1998. Five years later his story of fakery became a movie, *Shattered Glass*, starring Hayden Christensen as the faker. One also recalls Janet Cooke of the *Washington Post*, who in 1981 won a Pulitzer Prize for "Jimmy's World," about an eight-year-old heroin addict. The story turned out to be false, the newspaper apologized, and Cooke returned the Pulitzer. Even so, her fakery sparked interest from Tri-Star Pictures, which shelled out $1.6 million for the movie rights.

In May of 2008 Obama said he had campaigned in 57 states but the establishment media made nothing of it and the special treatment actually ramped up after the election. In April of 2009 the new President of the United States invented the "Austrian" language, apparently unaware that Austrians speak German. On the August 6, 2013 "Tonight Show" the president placed Charleston South Carolina, Jacksonville Florida and Savannah Georgia on the Gulf of Mexico, but that did not become a national story.

A credulous, establishment media in thrall to political correctness can hardly be expected to challenge the statist superstitions of any candidate, much less expose any Stalinist skeletons in the closet. Few in these circles show interest in the biggest mass movement of modern times, which prevailed in the largest nation on earth, the USSR. It still prevails in the most populous country on earth, China, and still thrives in places like North Korea and Cuba. Harvey Klehr and John Earl Haynes authored *Denial: Historians, Communism and Espionage* and other scholarly books, but in the old-line establishment media, ignorance of Communism is an asset and anti-Communism remains a cardinal sin. In these circles, all inquiries about American Communists amount to McCarthyism, xenophobia and paranoia.

Barry Rubin, who passed away in 2014, had a lot to say on this in *Silent Revolution: How the Left Rose to Political Power and Cultural Dominance*. A better title would be *Silent Counterrevolution* and with no apology to Gil Scott-Heron, this counterrevolution was televised.

As Rubin has it, the Third Left, an heir to the Old Left and New Left, took over liberalism and "put its emphasis on infiltrating the means of idea and opinion production," slandering the opposition in the style of Saul Alinsky and ignoring the failures of Communism. The Third Left goal was "to convince Americans the exact opposite of what their experience proved: that the country had fundamentally failed and the old leftist solutions were the answer."

For Rubin, the timing is significant.

"At the very moment in human history when it became obvious that the far left's ideas had failed and that statist, big-government, ever-higher-regulation policies did not work, it became possible for the first time ever to convince Americans that these things were precisely what the country needed." And in that cause, the old-line establishment media lent a hand.

Rubin cites the 2009 JournoList scandal, a project of former

Washington Post star pundit Ezra Klein. Influential writers, academics and members of the press on the confidential JournoList spoke of how to be most effective in ensuring Obama's election victory in 2008. That explains why, as Rubin says on page 133, "not a single serious investigation was conducted about Obama's earlier life." That earlier life remained shrouded in secrecy or decked out in disguise as in *Dreams from My Father*. Voters knew less about the man calling himself Barack Obama than any candidate in U.S. history, and this raises an issue.

Nobody gets in the FBI, the U.S. Marshals Service, or even a local police force by withholding academic transcripts, family documents and such. With Frank, the Kenyan Old Man, Lolo Soetoro, Gramps and Ann Dunham all dead, Madelyn Dunham, the candidate's maternal grandmother, was the person most in the know about the Democratic candidate. Reporters were not eager to seek her out, but she wasn't in the habit of talking to them. Madelyn Dunham passed away at 86 on November 3, 2008, one day before the election.

Interestingly enough, "Barack Obama's grandma, 86, dies of cancer before election," Dan Nakaso's story in the *Honolulu Advertiser*, cites Alice Dewey, Ann Dunham's graduate studies adviser and a family friend. Dewey says Madelyn Dunham was "always very affectionate with Ann and with Barry." Madelyn's death, Dewey said, was "just devastating for Barry," so the candidate's real name still had some staying power.

"We are five days away from fundamentally transforming the United States of America," proclaimed the candidate on October 30, 2008, in Columbia, Missouri.

On November 4, 2008, the candidate calling himself Barack Obama, became President of the United States, the most powerful man in the world, claiming a mandate to transform the nation. If this man was a liberal, as Barry Rubin wondered, why did he see a need fundamentally to transform a nation shaped by liberals such as Franklin Roosevelt with his New Deal and Lyndon Johnson with his Great Society?

As readers will recall, in *Dreams from My Father*, the author linked his career to his Kenyan father, the man of unsurpassed concentration who graduated in three years, became the first president of the

International Students Association, and went on to Harvard. In the early going as president, however, he showed little interest in Africa in general and Kenya in particular. Readers of *Dreams from My Father* might have expected the president to announce a massive Marshall Plan for the continent, with special attention to Kenya, that victim of racist British colonialism. The president did no such thing and made only one trip to Kenya, in July of 2015, when he joked about looking for his Kenyan birth certificate.

In the early going of his first term, the president did not seek any advisers from that nation, perhaps a relative, a colleague, or even one of the Kenyan's college professors. On the other hand, the president took strong affirmative action to tap the connections of Frank Marshall Davis.

In Chicago, Davis worked in Communist front groups with people such as Vernon Jarrett, whose son Dr. William Robert Jarrett married Valerie Bowman. She was the daughter of physician James Bowman, an active Communist with a lengthy FBI file. Valerie Bowman became Valerie Jarrett, who became the president's close adviser. The president is on record that she is like a sibling and that he trusts her completely. As it happens, Frank Marshall Davis also worked with Robert Rochon Taylor, maternal grandfather of Valerie Jarrett.

In his profile of David Axelrod as "Obama's narrator," Ben Wallace-Wells failed to note that Axelrod was a red diaper baby with strong connections to Chicago's old left. As Paul Kengor wrote in *The Communist*, Axelrod's mentor was David Canter, an old-line Stalinist who published Soviet propaganda and knew all about Frank Marshall Davis. So no surprise that the president brought Axelrod on board. He was, after all, the narrator.

Of all the president's advisors, Axelrod sat closest to the Oval Office, noted Jeff Zeleny in "President's Political Protector is Ever Close at Hand," a March 8, 2009 piece in the *New York Times*. "His voice, and political advice, carry more weight than most anyone else's on the president's payroll" and he describes himself as a protector of the president's image. "There are few words that come across the president's lips," wrote Zeleny, "that have not been blessed by Mr. Axelrod.

He reviews every speech, studies every major policy position and works with Robert Gibbs, the White House press secretary, to prepare responses to the crisis of the day."

So the president's inner circle showed zero influence from any Kenyan but plenty of sway from Frank. And old Gramps himself might wonder about the president's actions in office. On the foreign policy side, a number of issues demanded the president's attention but in one particular case he proceeded in a great hurry.

"I cannot honestly say that the voice in this book is not mine," says the narrator of this "useful fiction." But the author has "a stubborn desire to protect myself from scrutiny."

"Written with the narrative skill of a gifted novelist," explains David Axelrod, proclaimed "Obama's narrator" in the *New York Times*.

"The ghosts of Chicago's frightening political past are alive and well in Washington today," explains the professor.

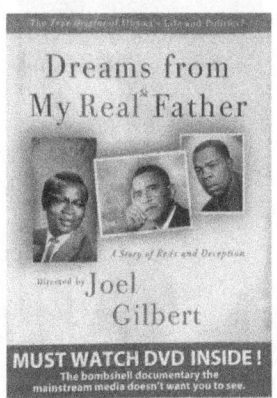

"You have the same mouth," said aunt Auma in *Dreams from My Father*.

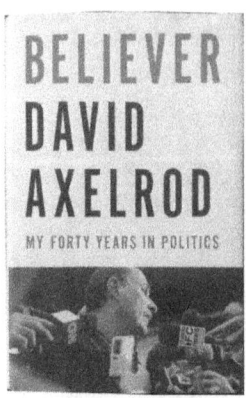

"I knew Barack was an exceptional writer," writes the president's narrator David Axelrod, a former journalist who "felt more comfortable, and proficient at, telling stories."

The "prop in someone else's narrative," from *Dreams from My Father*, who "bequeathed his name," is now the "other" Barack.

"The family myth contained a kind of truth," according to the *New York Times* reporter.

"Summer sessions at the university bring thousands of co-eds intent on having a ball," writes the author. "I have impregnated only three women, all white."

"I realize I would invite trouble if I named those with whom I have enjoyed supreme pleasure," wrote Frank Marshall Davis. "Therefore, I have changed names and identities."

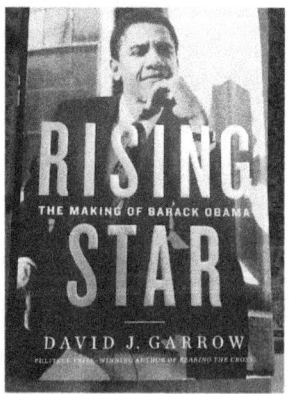

As the Pulitzer Prize winner explains, *Dreams from My Father* is "in multitudinous ways and without question a work of historical fiction," and the author a "composite character."

All photos by Lloyd Billingsley

"My heart is filled with love for this country."

In September, 2009, less than a year after his election victory, the President of the United States scrapped plans for an antiballistic missile shield in Eastern Europe. The *New York Times,* called it "one of the biggest security reversals of his young presidency," noting that the missile defense system was "fiercely opposed by Russia," which gave up nothing in the deal. The plan called for a radar facility in the Czech Republic and 10 ground based interceptors in Poland, nations that had been under the control of the Soviet Union during the Cold War.

In 1968, the Soviets invaded Czechoslovakia to crush the democratic reforms of the "Prague Spring." Frank Marshall Davis backed the Soviet invasion, as he did all phases of Soviet aggression, including the crackdown on the Solidarity dissidents in Poland. The president doubtless knew about Soviet repression of Eastern Europe, but recall that he said nothing about it in *Dreams from My Father*, where "dirty deeds" were the exclusive property of Ronald Reagan and his minions. Perhaps the president had forgotten about the Soviet invasion, just as he forgot everything the Kenyan Old Man said during a month-long visit.

In 2009, as at any time, Poland and the Czech Republic posed no threat to Russia, whose objections to the missile defense signaled a militant stance toward nations the USSR had controlled. Nothing readers have learned about the Kenyan would indicate that canceling missile defense was one of his dreams. The Kenyan Barack Obama, though a man of the left, never emerges as an apologist for the all-white Soviet Communist regime that colonized huge areas of Asia and occupied Eastern Europe for half a century. Indeed, Barack Obama warned his Kenyan countrymen about Soviet attempts to topple African governments. On the other hand, a full-speed rush to cancel missile defense would have been right in old Frank's wheelhouse.

During the Cold War, the American left fiercely opposed any attempt by the USA and its allies to defend against Soviet missile attack. The left derided such defense as "Star Wars" and charged that it would give the United States and the West an unfair advantage, or cover for a first strike. In similar style, Soviet and Communist Party front groups orchestrated movements for unilateral disarmament and a nuclear freeze that would lock in place Soviet advantages. These groups opposed U.S. deployments in Europe and smeared supporters of such moves as warmongers, right-wingers, xenophobes, militants, the familiar litany.

Emboldened by the president's cancelation of missile defense, Vladimir Putin, a former KGB man, duly invaded Ukraine, a sovereign nation, beginning with the Crimean peninsula. Beyond running his mouth, the President of the United States did nothing to stop this Russian aggression. Frank would have the president's back on that one.

Back in the day, Frank regarded Russians as the "niggers of the globe," and had never objected to anything Stalin had done in Ukraine, including the murder of millions through forced famine, a tactic Stalin pioneered. But then, Frank never objected to anything Stalin and the all-white Soviet regime did at any time. With "Pop" Frank the poet, the white Soviet bosses always knew best. For Frank and the rest of the American left, the United States and its allies were the evil empire. And Frank's zeal for arms limitation did not apply to the Soviet Union.

On July 20, 1946, Frank Marshall Davis wrote a column headlined, "A-Bombs for Russia," part of the Communist Party's push for Stalin to get nuclear weapons, before his spies stole the plans from the United States. The current President of the United States is celebrating a deal that gives Iran the right to inspect its own nuclear facilities and provides a month's warning for outside inspections. For this deal, as for other programs and policies, the administration enjoyed full collaboration from the establishment media and commentariat.

"We created an echo chamber," Ben Rhodes, the president's Deputy

National Security Advisor for Strategic Communications, told David Samuels of the *New York Times Magazine*. "They were saying things that validated what we had given them to say." In Samuels' May 5, 2016 piece, "The Aspiring Novelist Who Became Obama's Foreign-Policy Guru," Rhodes also explained that newspapers no longer have foreign bureaus, and that "the average reporter we talk to is 27 years old, and their only reporting experience consists of being around political campaigns. That's a sea change. They literally know nothing."

So know-nothing reporters willingly serve as an echo chamber, even on a deal that, as more than a few experts believe, virtually guarantees that Iran will acquire nuclear weapons. The president clearly regards this as a major achievement, but readers will find no indication that such a thing was ever a dream of the Kenyan Barack Obama.

Frank, meanwhile, was very active after World War II, when Stalin grabbed Eastern Europe, including half of Germany. That became the German Democratic Republic (GDR), a one-party Communist totalitarian dictatorship and with the possible exception of Bulgaria the Soviets' most slavish ally in the region. Frank was still in his prime in August, 1961, when the Communist regime threw up the Berlin Wall to keep Germans from fleeing to freedom in the West. Thousands attempted to escape and hundreds died trying. Frank was a vocal supporter of all Soviet colonies and the East German Stasi, the "Red Gestapo" as inmates called it, drew no objection from the eager columnist.

On June 12, 1987, Ronald Reagan challenged Soviet boss Mikhail Gorbachev to "tear down this wall." Frank was around until July 26, 1987, so he likely knew about the speech. He hated the anti-Communist Reagan, as they say, with a passion, but the old Stalinist would have been more perturbed on November 9, 1989, when the wall came tumbling down and the inmates were free at last. That proved unsettling to Vladimir Putin, whose first KGB posting had been East Germany. Putin's role had been to keep that nation captive to Soviet power and to repress the German people. After the Berlin Wall came down, Moscow under Mikhail Gorbachev did not send in the tanks, as in Hungary in 1956 and Czechoslovakia in 1968. So Putin and other KGB thugs burned up evidence of their work before retreating to the Soviet

Fatherland. Unfortunately, the Soviet oppressors were never held to account in any kind of Nuremberg trial.

Twenty-five years later, in 2014, Europeans celebrated the Berlin Wall's collapse. The most notable no-show was the President of the United States, whose book mentioned Reagan's "dirty deeds" but not those of a single totalitarian regime, not even East Germany, one of the worst. The November 7, 2014, White House Statement on the 25th anniversary did not mention the USSR, Communism, or totalitarianism, and even failed to name the so-called German Democratic Republic. The statement refers to "oppressive regimes" but gives no detail of how oppressive the GDR actually was. The White House statement says the wall separated Germans "from family and friends" and that Germans were "trying to escape to freedom." But the president gives no detail on what conditions the brave Germans sought to escape.

Besides the Stasi repression, the GDR had nothing resembling the private sector in Western democracies. The state ran everything, and its command economy guaranteed that the GDR would be an economic basket case, less consequential to the world economy than Hong Kong. So the Germans were fleeing state-enforced poverty as well as political repression. They knew from experience that the command economy doesn't work and has never worked, the direct opposite of what Frank and the President of the United States believed.

The Kenyan Old Man, an "anti-colonialist" in the default media description, was in Hawaii when the East German regime built the Berlin Wall. He is not on record supporting such a move and never emerges as a slavish supporter of the GDR in the style of Frank.

In his second term, the President of the United States normalized relations with Cuba, a former Soviet colony and one of the most repressive regimes in the world, headed by one of the most loathsome dictators. Fidel Castro, a sadist, Stalinist and economic crackpot, has been in power since the 1950s and driven a formerly prosperous nation to sub-Haiti levels of poverty. As Nestor Almendros showed in *Improper Conduct*, the white Castro dictatorship repressed writers and artists, persecuted homosexuals, punished dissidents, and maintains many black political prisoners. Like East Germany, the regime kills those who attempt to leave, making the Florida Straits a cemetery without crosses.

The Castro regime, which hosted deployment of Soviet missiles in the early 1960s, was not becoming more open or less militant. In 2014, the regime tried to ship 240 tons of weapons to North Korea, including two Soviet MiG-21 fighters, air defense systems, missiles and command-and-control vehicles. Cuba had also been on the list of nations that sponsors terrorism. For normalizing relations with this totalitarian Communist regime, the President of the United States got absolutely nothing by way of democratic reforms, just as he got nothing by canceling missile defense in Europe. He never took up the cause of a single Cuban dissident or writer. It was okay with the president that Communist dictators Fidel and Raul Castro remain in power.

The Kenyan Old Man never showed enthusiasm for the Cuban dictator and his one-party regime, which became not only a Soviet colony in the Americas but the Soviets' foreign legion in Africa, with 25,000 troops in Angola in 1975. On the other hand, Frank was a big fan of white dictator Fidel Castro and a Soviet colony on America's doorstep was one of his dreams, as was a Soviet America.

"I pledge myself to rally the masses to defend the Soviet Union, the land of victorious socialism," reads the oath Frank swore. "I pledge myself to remain at all times a vigilant and firm defender of the Leninist line of the Party, the only line that insures the triumph of Soviet Power in the United States." So Frank would back the president's Cuba move 100 percent.

In May, 2016, the president paid a visit to Vietnam, still a one-party Communist dictatorship that denies basic human rights. The president took the occasion to criticize the United States for economic inequality and racial bias in the criminal justice system. The president claimed that the United States had "shared ideals" with Ho Chi Minh, a Stalinist, and seemed to chart a moral equivalence, lamenting that people had died on "both sides" of the conflict. He did not recall the re-education camps, the Boat People, or anything like that.

Silent Revolution author Barry Rubin was unable to find a single case where the president criticized any leftist movement or Third

World leftist dictator. Likewise, he has never criticized Marxism or Communism in principle, never assessed their economic failures, and never discussed their repressions.

In *Dreams from My Father*, the author evokes the lost hopes of Communists, then sulking in the loser's locker room. His actions as president recall the men's basketball final at the 1972 Olympics in Munich. The United States, with their youngest squad ever, won the game fair and square against an older and more experienced Soviet team. As they celebrated, Renato William Jones, secretary general of FIBA, International Federation of Amateur Basketball, came out of the stands and prevailed on Olympic officials to put time back on the clock, three times. On the third try, the Soviets scored a basket, taking away the American victory.

In similar style, the president nixes hard-won victories of the West by cancelling missile defense for American allies, a "security reversal" as the *New York Times* called it. He puts time back on the clock for Cuba's white Stalinist dictators, Fidel and Raul Castro. Frank would have loved it, but the influence did not end there.

Frank Marshall Davis, an African American poet, backed a white Soviet Communist regime that censored the poetry of Boris Pasternak and did not allow publication of his 1957 novel *Doctor Zhivago* until 1988, more than 20 years after the 1965 *Doctor Zhivago* film. Frank Marshall Davis the journalist backed a totalitarian regime that controlled all news and information.

The author of *Dreams from My Father* speaks of a "stubborn desire to protect myself from scrutiny." So it makes sense that his administration, which he proclaimed the most transparent in history, turned out to be the most opaque and obstructionist. Based on his own record, Frank would have applauded the way the president managed the press.

On his watch, the president of CBS news was David Rhodes brother of Ben Rhodes, a top national security advisor to Obama and up to his eyeballs in the Benghazi scandal. Joel Molinoff, a veteran of the NSA, came to CBS after serving the Obama White House as director for President's Intelligence Advisory Board. CBS also hired Mike Morell formerly a deputy director at the CIA and a major figure in Benghazi.

So as Sharyl Attkisson explained in *Stonewalled: My Fight for Truth Against the Forces of Obstruction, Intimidation, and Harassment in Obama's Washington*, many CBS stories might as well have been written by the White House.

Attkisson, a liberal, probed the "Fast and Furious" and Benghazi scandals, among others. She describes working at her computer when something takes over and starts wiping out material. She has the presence of mind to grab her phone and shoot a video. She finds that her computer has been infiltrated by means of spyware proprietary to government agencies such as the CIA, FBI and NSA, conducting surveillance against all Americans. She also finds the intruders planted classified information on her computer. That adds "the possible threat of criminal prosecution" to the author's list of delay, denial, obstruction, intimidation, retaliation, bullying, and surveillance from the supposedly transparent Obama administration. So the president not only throws up a Berlin Wall against curious reporters but transforms U.S. intelligence and law enforcement agencies into a veritable American Stasi deployed on the domestic scene.

By all accounts, the Kenyan Barack H. Obama was a man who never hesitated to speak his mind, and that candor landed him in trouble with the Kenyan government. Readers might try to find anybody of note who believes that high-tech harassment of journalists was a dream of the Kenyan Barack Obama. Consider also government linkage of dissenters with terrorists.

Challengers from the Sidelines: Understanding America's Violent Far-Right came out in 2013 from the Combating Terrorism Center at West Point, the U.S. Military Academy. The author, Arlie Perlinger, had no background in terrorism and the study purports to deal with white supremacists, Aryan Nations, skinheads, the Ku Klux Klan and such. Members of these groups "espouse strong convictions regarding the federal government, believing it to be corrupt and tyrannical, with a natural tendency to intrude on individuals' civil and constitutional rights. Finally, they support civil activism, individual freedoms, and self-government." As journalist Mark Tapson noted, "that pretty much describes every conservative I know." The sub-text is clear.

Those Americans less than worshipful about ever-expanding and intrusive government, who value their constitutional rights, and dare to participate in civil activism, are dangerous subversives.

If your views are different from those of the president, you become a "subversive mother," like Fielding Melish in Woody Allen's 1971 film *Bananas*. Frank, who attacked anyone less than worshipful of Stalin, would have no problem with that, nor with the president's style of ruling by executive order. Like Gramps, readers might recall those "principles that promised a higher form of power," from *Dreams from My Father*. In practice this amounts to higher than the rule of law, and beyond accountability to the other branches of government. This is more like Frank and the principles he espoused. For his part, the Kenyan Barack H. Obama clearly had issues with strong-man types such as Jomo Kenyatta, who ruled Kenya from independence in 1963 until his death in 1978.

The Kenyan Barack Obama was a contentious, argumentative type but he never comes across as a hater in the style of Frank, who said that "black people have a reason to hate." The president is chummy with hatemongering groups such as "Black Lives Matter" and charlatans like Al Sharpton. And the president has never disowned the hateful Reverend Wright.

On the president's watch, the old CPUSA and Comintern concept of a separate black nation in the American south started getting some traction. The Kenyan Barack Obama never backed anything like that, but Frank the Stalinist would have been on board with black-belt apartheid.

Meanwhile, the Kenyan Barack Obama went to Harvard to study economic development and trade, hardly indicative of opposition to the free market. According to Sally Jacobs, author of *The Other Barack: The Bold and Reckless Life of President Obama's Father*, the Kenyan titled his PhD thesis "An Econometric Model of Staple Theory of Development." Staple theory explains economic development in areas with abundant natural resources and a relatively small population. It is not a favorite theory of Marxist economists and does not indicate hostility to free enterprise or foreign investment. In Auma's account in *Dreams from My Father*, the Old Man worked for an American oil company, Shell. So the Kenyan's economic and political profile is decidedly different than Frank's.

If you have a business, the president says, you didn't build that and somebody else made it happen. If you like your health plan you can keep it, the president said. Except that you can't. Under the president's model, you don't get what you want. You get only what the government wants you to have. That's part of the fundamental transformation from a country with a government to a government with a country. That is more like the totalitarian model Frank promoted than anything that emerged from the Kenyan Barack Obama. Dead since 1982, he was now, as Sally Jacobs titled her 2011 biography, *The Other Barack.*

The last page of *The Other Barack* explains that Peter Osnos founded the Public Affairs publishing house in 1997 as a tribute to three people. The first is I.F. Stone, billed as "one of the great independent journalists in American history." Stone is the author of *The Hidden History of the Korean War*, which charges that South Korea attacked North Korea, the reverse of what happened. As John Earl Haynes, Harvey Klehr and Alexander Vassiliev note in *Spies: The Rise and Fall of the KGB in America*, I.F. Stone took money from the KGB, so he was neither great nor independent, any more than Frank Marshall Davis was great or independent. The ad copy on Stone supports Barry Rubin's contention that the left "put its emphasis on infiltrating the means of idea and opinion production."

The Other Barack author Sally Jacobs, a *Boston Globe* reporter, regards *Dreams from My Father* as (page 134), "a heartfelt rumination on his relationship with his absent father." His "paternal roots lie in far-away Africa" and she quotes *Dreams* uncritically, avoiding such troublesome details as the author's need to avoid scrutiny, the voice in the book, the prop, and the useful fiction. On the other hand, Jacobs brings new information to light.

For example (page 84), Obama the candidate repeatedly claimed his Kenyan father was part of the first airlift of foreign students. Jacobs found this claim to be untrue. Not only was the Kenyan Barack Obama not a member of the first airlift, he was in fact turned down for it, with good reason. He had earned only a third-division pass for the

Cambridge School Certificate, the lowest possible score to advance. *Dreams from My Father* contends that the Kenyan "won another scholarship, this time to pursue his PhD at Harvard." And when he shows up in Kenya, a Miss Omoro asks: "You wouldn't be related to Dr. Obama by any chance?"

In reality, the Kenyan never earned a PhD but duly described himself as "Doctor." That profile might be at odds with the foreign student of unsurpassed concentration, "the brilliant scholar, the generous friend, the upstanding leader" of *Dreams from My Father*.

Jacobs charts how, in Massachusetts, the Kenyan spent money on women, not Barack Obama Jr. back in Hawaii, who was called "Barry" by the people Jacobs interviewed. Harvard eventually withdrew support for the Kenyan and, in effect, gave him the boot. Jacobs has also been into B.H. Obama's immigration file, and notes that he was forced to leave Cambridge, Massachusetts, against his will, in 1964.

As Jacobs learned, Barack Obama's whiskey guzzling got him tagged "double-double." He was known for drunken rages and (page 231) threatened to kill his wife Ruth Baker, the white American woman he married in 1965. Barack Obama left three wives in his wake and five or seven children. Like Auma, Jacobs remains unsure about many details because Kenyans' accounts of Barack Obama show wide variation. As Toby Harnden of the *Telegraph* wrote in a review of Jacobs' book, Barack Obama was a "drunkard and a professional failure," who "achieved almost nothing." He was an "inveterate liar, a sponger and a braggart," and "little short of a monster" for his violence toward women. Whatever his qualities or defects, by 2011 he was the "other" Barack. The one who mattered was in the White House, the President of the United States, the most powerful man in the world. To speak his name is to validate the useful fiction in *Dreams from My Father*.

Though Jacobs apparently regards the book as infallible, the reporter did not indulge any speculation about Frank. The old Stalinist is absent from Jacobs' account, as he is from *The Audacity of Hope*, the audio version of *Dreams*, and a lot of other writing about the president. Such omissions are not accidental and hugely significant. Frank had been a key figure and, unlike the Kenyan Old Man, the author seemed to have forgotten not a single thing Frank ever said, right down to pronouncements on women, such as: "They'll drive you to drink, boy, and if you let 'em, they'll drive you into your grave."

Also unlike the Kenyan Barack Obama, Frank left a vast record of writings. Like Gramps, readers might be interested in what Frank had to say on the touchy subject of fatherhood.

"Quite a few coeds are available for special affairs."

As Frank often lamented, journalism is not a high-paying profession, and the Communist Party USA, though very demanding on the work side, was notoriously cheap when it came to paying the workers. Davis did what his white CPUSA bosses required of him, but no surprise that he should strive to supplement his income.

In his *Livin' the Blues* memoir, Frank talks up his interest in photography. He acquires a camera and darkroom equipment and starts shooting models.

"As I gained confidence behind the lens, I turned to nudes," Frank writes (page 230), "Obviously, the female body fascinates me, both aesthetically and emotionally. The steatopygian aspect (I use the word advisedly) of black women pleases me; lack of another outstanding (another apt adjective) derriere is my chief complaint against the majority of Caucasian women. However, brown thighs are sometimes too heavy proportionately for my personal idea of beauty. But other attributes being desirable, I never let that stop me. If breasts, waist, legs and face were pleasing, I simply posed them to minimize bad features and accentuated the positive."

Long before *Playboy,* Hugh Hefner, and the sexual revolution, Frank had no trouble acquiring subjects.

"I was amazed at the number of gals eager to strip and stand unclothed before the all-seeing eye of the camera. Sometimes husbands brought their wives to pose nude – apparently so that in later years when mates developed middle-aged spread they could look back with graphic nostalgia on what used to be." His friend Thelma, "had no hesitancy about asking a shapely girl to have her picture taken with nothing on her but lights."

In May of 1946, Frank writes (page 299), "I crossed the color line to marry Helen, the blonde student from my jazz class. She was eighteen years my junior and looked like a model." Helen Canfield was indeed a stately, striking figure, with flowing blond hair. *Livin' the Blues* shows the happy couple smiling and in that 1947 shot an upscale 35mm camera dangles around Frank's neck. If he took nude photos of Helen they have not surfaced, but there was more to the relationship than physical attraction and love of jazz. Helen Canfield was also a member of the Communist Party USA. Marrying within the Party was common practice, and Helen went along when Party bosses shipped Frank to Hawaii in 1948. *Livin' the Blues* shows Frank and Helen Davis in Honolulu in 1949, decked out in matching dark Hawaiian shirts. They stand proudly with their first child, Lynn, in front of the *Honolulu Record* where Frank worked.

As Frank notes in *Livin' the Blues*, the cost of living in Hawaii is high. While working three shifts for the Party, Frank started the Oahu Paper Company, which burned down in 1952. After that, he started the Paradise Paper Company, without much success. As John Edgar Tidwell of Miami (Ohio) University explains in his introduction to Davis' memoir, "economic reversals forced him to take up the pen for purely monetary reasons." The result was the 1968 *Sex Rebel: Black*, subtitled *Memoirs of a Gash Gourmet,* published by Greenleaf Classics in San Diego, which churned out classics such as *After Wife Swapping? Aphrodisiac, Daddy's Girl*, and *The Orgies of Stone's Island*, by, respectively, Robert Bonfils, Sebastion Gray, Kyle Roxbury, and R. John Smyth, whose identities may well be doubted. Greenleaf publisher Donald H. Gilmore is the likely author of the introductions under such names as Del Grayson (for *Partygirl*, another classic), Douglas Gamlin and Dale Gordon Phd, author of the introduction to *Sex Rebel: Black*.

Tidwell describes Frank's work as a "soft-core pornographic novel." Hard-core would be more like it, though in the Internet age, when one click can summon virtually anything, the term has lost meaning. Scholars and journalists alike have shied away from Frank's account, perhaps for the same reason the *Dreams* author had declined to visit Kenya. "Maybe I'm scared of what I'll find out," he explained.

Readers might have some fun reading passages aloud, but they would do better to see it as a confessional. Davis used the pseudonym Bob Greene, but *Sex Rebel: Black* is clearly all about Frank, who owned up to writing it. In this tale, true to form, the author comes up in Chicago and in 1950 moves to Hawaii. It's not an openly political book but Frank can't help but tip his hand. In places he begins a sentence with "Frankly," an allusion to his "Frankly Speaking" newspaper columns. On page 115, he explains, with the Soviet Union and the United States allies in the world struggle against the Axis, "it was respectable to join and work with many groups later labeled Communist."

On page 185 he explains that Charlene, one of his sexual conquests, and like him a lover of jazz, is of "French-Italian descent" and that Charlene's mother was "ultraconservative, an admirer of Hitler and Mussolini and hated both Jews and Negroes." Even so, Bob and Charlene become a couple, and she bears his children. Charlene is doubtless a stand-in for Helen Canfield, the white Communist Party USA member Frank married in May of 1946.

"I'm black," the author explains in the foreword. "Well, not exactly black. It's more medium brown, but since my ancestry is predominantly African, I'm considered black." And he has been swinging and swapping, he writes, since 1937.

"In addition to cunnilingus, at times I enjoy analingus," the author tells readers right up front. "I often wish I had two penises to enjoy simultaneously the sensations of oral and genital copulation." On the other hand, "I realize I would invite trouble if I named those with whom I have enjoyed supreme pleasure." Therefore, says the author (page 14), "I have changed names and identities. However, all incidents I have described were taken from actual experiences," and the author gives readers ample reason to believe him.

Though he has changed names and identities, readers won't find anything like the "I cannot honestly say that the voice in this book is not mine," dodge from *Dreams from My Father*. This is Frank his own self, a man "vastly experienced," as Roscoe Lee Browne said in *The Cowboys*.

"I do like white women, along with black women too," the author explains. But "what amazed me is that, despite numerous black partners, I have impregnated white women only – and just two of them." One is clearly Charlene and Frank leaves clues about the other, even though he has "changed names and identities."

As it happens, Ann Dunham, the president's mother, was set on attending the University of Washington when her parents moved to Hawaii. The sudden move yanked Ann away from her friends and threw her into a stage of rebellion, particularly against her father. He is supposedly a furniture salesman but the U.S. Army veteran had been photographed wearing the insignia of Notre Dame de Jamhour, a French language school in Beirut, Lebanon. For Boston University emeritus professor Angelo Codevilla, a U.S. Navy and foreign service vet, that hints at intelligence connections. Most likely, Stanley was keeping an eye on Frank for the U.S. government. Stanley's rebellious daughter Ann, short on friends in a strange place, came to enjoy Frank's company. In due time, she posed nude for Frank, who sold the photos to magazines. In the course of these sessions Frank had sex with Ann and impregnated her. Then the family later contrived to name the Kenyan Barack Obama as the father, and the legend grew from there. *Sex Rebel: Black* lends support to this scenario.

The author encounters (page 274) Lloyd and Dorothy, a swinging couple from Seattle, interestingly enough. Lloyd tells the author that "quite a few coeds are available for special affairs" and "for the most part it's posing nude for photographs." The author encounters an underage girl named Anne. This is in Chicago but the author tells readers he has changed things around lest he invite trouble. Anne is supposedly a Jamaican teen, 13, who lost her virginity at 12, and sex with the author is her idea, not his. In fact, she is "chomping at the bit" to get on with it.

"I'm not one to go in for Lolitas," the author explains, and "rarely for teenagers." However, "there are exceptions. I didn't want to disappoint the trusting child. At her age a rejection might be traumatic, could even cripple her sexually for life. No, I didn't want anything like that on my conscience." So he agrees, and on page 74 explains:

"Dressed, she looked like a child with great potential; nude you realized she was as physically mature as many young women. At rest, her face was unusually sensual and she had a peculiar way of curving the right side of her mouth when she smiled. Her hair – long, thick, shiny black and straight – reached her waist. But it was her bosom and generally shapeliness that gassed me. Her loose child's clothing gave no hint of her beautifully formed breasts. They'd grow bigger as she grew older but could never become more appealing. She'd also fill out more in the hips in years to come, but even now I could find no flaw in her figure."

The black straight hair is not what one would expect from a Jamaican girl with skin the color of "antique gold." The detailed facial description is absent from Bob's other encounters and the rest bears some similitude to Ann Dunham around 1960. Her clothing is indeed loose and hardly revealing, but the nude photos Frank Marshall Davis published confirm what the author observed. She was indeed "physically mature as many young women." And the photographer, experienced with nudes, knew how to minimize bad features and accentuate the positive.

The author says that around the age of 55 he began to wonder whether he was still attractive to women. Frank Marshall Davis was 55 in 1960, and an eager coed could be just the ticket to feel good about himself. Other parts of the narrative also prove revealing.

Molly, an Australian lady, cautions the author, "You will withdraw at the proper time, won't you? I have no protection." The author admits he is not a fan of condoms. Before servicing Alice Lanier, an attractive widow from Butte, Montana, the author says, "I didn't want her to be the third white woman I had knocked up." *Sex Rebel: Black* does not say Anne became pregnant, but then the author admits up front that he changed names and identities so he would not invite trouble. That Ann Dunham was indeed knocked up is undeniable. And *Sex Rebel: Black* confirms why, beyond his Stalinist politics, her offspring and his handlers would want to cover up any connection with the man who acknowledged writing it.

As a teenager, the author explains (page 40), "I had the unique experience of fellating my own prick until I shot off in my own mouth. This was real do-it-yourself cocksucking, complete self-service." And as an adult, in certain circumstances, the author writes, "I enjoy sucking another man's cock." So Frank even surpasses the hero of *Shaft*, played by Richard Roundtree. Frank is a sex machine for all the chicks and guys alike. For Frank, it doesn't matter who he loves.

Readers may perceive here what the author of *Dreams from My Father* meant by the "less flattering aspects of my father's character," and perhaps another reason for that "stubborn desire to protect myself from scrutiny."

As they say, the first step in getting what you want is knowing what it is. Frank knew what he wanted.

"I prefer a woman with abundant pubic hair," the black sex rebel explains (page 36). "I like the sense of power I feel in bringing a woman to orgasm." Sometime during his Hawaii sojourn, the author met Gwen, whom he dubbed (page 320) "Gwen the Chick with the Cavernous Cunt," and sometimes "Old Tunnel Twat." Analingus and anal sex with a woman named Dot prompts this meditation:

"It's funny about an asshole," the author writes (page 301). "The sphincter muscles are unusually strong and in response it's far tighter than a cunt. Yet it can take a cock just as easily as can a pussy, especially after conditioning. I worked my pole up her educated pit within seconds."

Frank clearly favored a sort of "plug and play" approach. Near the end, when he is 62, he explains:

"I'm as hungry as I ever was for Hedy LaMarr, Joan Crawford, Ginger Rogers, Dolores Del Rio, and Marlene Dietrich." And he finds Peggy Lee and Barbara Stanwyck "far more appealing than 25 years go."

As Peggy Lee said, chicks were made to give you fever, Fahrenheit or centigrade. Frank still had the fever. He was probably having fun at that point, and happy for the extra cash, but it would be no joke for Ann Dunham. And terms of endearment such as "Old Tunnel Twat" and "Cavern Cunt" might not find favor with Democratic Party activists, professors of feminist studies at UC Santa Barbara, and readers in general.

Though long out of print, *Sex Rebel: Black* did make a comeback of sorts on Amazon, which offered a print copy for the rather lofty price of $275. A five-star review posted on October 14, 2008, said the book "is believed to be the work of the poet Frank Marshall Davis," and that the Barack Obama campaign had confirmed that "Frank" from *Dreams from My Father* "is in fact the same person."

Readers should also consider that some passages from the 1968 *Sex Rebel: Black* show up in *Livin' the Blues*, which came out in 1992, five years after Davis died.

Frank is an only child who quickly learns that "grown-ups must put their mouths down there. . . Frankly, I was proud of myself for solving this strange riddle. And more significantly, this undoubtedly triggered my lifelong oral orientation; it had to start somewhere."

Frank and his friends "all knew what it meant to jazz a Jane, whip that jellyroll to a fare-thee-well, get a piece of tail or ass." According to Frank (page 36), "women had a cock" and "since our meaning of the key word was the exact opposite of common parlance, a cocksucker logically engaged in cunnilingus."

Readers might run a search for references to "cocksucker" as one who engages in cunnilingus. In *Livin' the Blues*, with his real name on the cover, Frank is trying to change the story, but he still explains that he and his friends "knew what happened when someone gobbled the goo." Someone with male and female characteristics was a "morfy-dyke, a bulldagger" who screwed other women just like a man. And "all such people, incidentally, were freaks." Both books cite sexologist Alfred Kinsey, and Frank finds common cause with the gay community. Consider this passage, for example:

"Contemporary American society still treats homosexuals as it does other unpopular minorities such as blacks – with hate, scorn and discrimination," wrote Davis on page 206 of *Livin' the Blues*. "During the dramatic civil rights demonstrations of the 1960s, I often thought we ought to form a united front with joint sit-ins at cafes. In my mind I envisioned the result. An indignant white restaurant manager frantically phoning the police, 'Get here in a hurry! We got niggers at our counters and our washrooms are loaded with fairies and lesbians!' Or perhaps there might have been a joint March on Washington waving banners: Blacks and Homos, Arise!"

This might be worth pondering. In Frank's time, very few black men were willing to equate the civil rights movement with the homosexual cause. After all, as far as scholars know, homosexuals were not brought to America in slave ships from any homosexual country in Africa. So Frank's commitment to the homosexual cause was perhaps stronger than he let on, and it had consequences down the line.

As a U.S. Senator, Barack Obama opposed the legalization of gay marriage. In 2012, during his second term as President of the United States, he changed his position and supported the right of same-sex couples to marry. Nothing that has emerged about the Kenyan Barack Obama indicates that such a move was one of his dreams. Indeed, to put it mildly, Kenya, like many African countries, looks askance at homosexuality. Of the more than 50 countries in Africa, only South Africa has legalized same-sex marriage. When the U.S. Supreme Court legalized gay marriage, Zimbabwe's president Robert Mugabe, not known as a barrel of laughs, quipped that he would propose marriage to president Obama.

On his only trip to Kenya in 2015, the American president talked up gay rights but Kenyan president Uhuru Kenyatta called that a "non-issue" and changed the subject. On the other hand, Frank Marshall Davis would have had the president's back on this one. Blacks and homos, one in the spirit. That was one of his dreams, and readers would do well to ponder carefully a few other passages from his work.

In *Sex Rebel: Black*, for example, the eager Molly is an Australian tourist. In *Livin' the Blues*, Frank notes that "white female tourists have a yen for these 'boys,'" some past the age of fifty.

In *Sex Rebel: Black,* coeds are pining for a good time. In *Livin the Blues* (page 317), "summer sessions at the university bring thousands of co-eds intent on having a ball," and "goodly numbers of Caucasian females shed their inhibitions." Hawaii is a paradise with some of the most beautiful women on earth and "Afro-American brothers make out with all kinds of dolls." A black African from Ghana (page 318), "wreaked havoc among coeds." And "another student from Kenya split leaving two pregnant blondes."

So in Frank Marshall Davis' official memoir, published by the

University of Wisconsin Press, a Kenyan student duly shows up Hawaii. Readers might recall that in *Dreams from My Father*, the author's father was "a prop in someone else's narrative." He doesn't blame his mother or grandparents for this, noting: "My father may have preferred the image they created for him – indeed, he may have been complicit in its creation."

Readers might want to give that some thought. Since Frank is clearly the "Pop" in the author's poem, the simplest explanation is that the old Stalinist was in on the theft of the Kenyan's identity and fully comfortable with the story. The Kenyan Barack Obama died in 1982 and Frank was around until 1987. The unnamed Kenyan in his memoir supposedly knocked up two unidentified blonds, but Frank is well aware of his own record.

"Strange as it may seem," he writes in *Livin' the Blues* (page 333), "I have impregnated only three women, all white. One had a miscarriage and the second an abortion." Frank supplies no names for any of the three pregnant ladies, but it is certainly possible to guess. Curious readers may find other clues in Ann's story.

"A kind of truth."

The definitive treatment of the president's mother, Ann Dunham, comes from *New York Times* reporter Janny Scott, whose *A Singular Woman: The Untold Story of Barack Obama's Mother* from Riverhead Books appeared in 2011, the same year as Sally Jacobs' *The Other Barack*. Readers may find it significant that Scott's book has no index and that the epigraph is from the preface to the 2004 edition of *Dreams from My Father*:

"I think sometimes that had I known she would not survive her illness, I might have written a different book – less a meditation on the absent parent, more a celebration of the one who was the single constant in my life."

As *Dreams from My Father* makes clear, she was not the single constant in his life, far from it. The epigraph to the preface is also of interest.

"I am the son of a black man from Kenya and a white woman from Kansas," Barack Obama, March 18, 2008.

With an introduction like that, readers are unlikely to find any challenge to the president's official story. Scott is aware of the controversies but instead of probing the issues, the *New York Times* reporter opts for quick and glib dismissal:

"And in the fevered imaginings of supermarket tabloids and the Internet," Scott writes (page 2), "she is the atheist, the Marxist, the flower child, the mother who 'abandoned' her son or duped the state of Hawaii into issuing a birth certificate for her Kenyan-born baby on the off chance that he might want to be president someday."

Scott, in effect, adds to the controversy, and the title of her book is already misleading.

Anyone writing about Ann Dunham, Scott explains (page 6), must address the question of what to call her. She was Stanley Ann Dunham at birth and Stanley as a child. She dropped Stanley after high school. Then came Ann Dunham, then Ann Obama then Ann Soetoro until her second divorce. She modified that name to Sutoro and in the early 80s she was Ann Sutoro, Ann Dunham Sutoro and S. Ann Dunham Sutoro on her dissertation. So she wasn't exactly a "singular" woman, and Scott opts to call her "whatever name she was using at the time." Among those, "Obama" is definitely outnumbered.

Scott's main source is "President Obama's sweet and lyrical *Dreams from My Father*, woven from tales he was told as a child." In that book, Scott notes (page 41), Obama writes that his mother was born at Fort Leavenworth, the Army base where Stanley was stationed. But Scott learns that Ralph Dunham, Stanley's older brother, said he visited mother Madelyn and her baby in Wichita Hospital when the child was a day or two old. So it wasn't Fort Leavenworth. And mother Ann would later say, "she had nearly entered the world in a speeding taxi." The author does not note when she said this, nor to whom.

Scott gives some background on Hawaii and the East-West Center the U.S. federal government established there "to exchange ideas, information and beliefs through cooperative study," with advisers including UN undersecretary Ralph J. Bunche.

Maya, Ann's daughter with the Indonesian Lolo Soetoro, told Scott (page 80), "We often would say that Mom met her husband at the East-West Center," while conceding, Scott adds, "that it was not strictly true." The Kenyan student Barack Obama was not on an East-West Center grant and in fact the center had not yet been built. So what they would say was in fact false, "but the family myth contained a kind of truth," the *New York Times* reporter explains. "Wherever Ann and Obama met, it was in a moment suffused with the spirit in which the center was born."

Like Gramps, readers might wonder about "a kind of truth." Could a witness in a murder trial swear to tell "a kind of truth," for example? Consider a Declaration of Independence that hailed "a kind of truth" to be self-evident. Would the author undergo an operation by someone whose claim to a medical degree was not strictly true?

Since Maya's admission comes from an actual family member, readers might wonder if other accounts of how the couple met were "not strictly true" or possibly just suffused with "a kind of truth."

One friend, whom Scott does not name (page 81), "said he remembered Ann saying she met Obama in the library," but according to the younger Obama, "they met in a Russian language class." Scott leaves it to the reader to decide which account in the family myth is true, or a kind of truth.

The Kenyan Barack Obama arrives one month after Hawaii's statehood, with 80 other Kenyans, sponsored by Kenyan nationalist Tom Mboya. Obama is "charismatic and sharp" and to Americans "his accent suggested Oxbridge, and his booming baritone voice brought to mind Paul Robeson."

The Robeson comparison is interesting, but not a direct quote from anybody Scott interviewed. In the sweet, lyrical *Dreams from My Father*, neither Ann Dunham nor the author describe the Kenyan's voice as a booming baritone that brought to mind Paul Robeson. Gramps might think he looks like Nat King Cole, but Gramps is not on record that he sounds like Paul Robeson. Of course, the author can't remember a single thing the Kenyan said during an entire month, but he does remember that Frank was a comrade of Paul Robeson. As it happens, Frank Marshall Davis, though less talented, did have a deep voice like Robeson's.

Scott cites accounts from graduate students such as Pake Zane, Chet Gorman and Neil Abercrombie. Also cited is Richard Hook who worked with Obama years later in Kenya. By all accounts he was smart and charismatic, a straight-A student who commanded attention when he spoke. None of the students and colleagues, however, describe the Kenyan as a fan of American jazz, Dave Brubeck, or rock and roll, which *Dreams from My Father* takes such pains to establish. And as Scott says "not everyone was charmed" by the man.

Some found Obama arrogant, egotistical and overbearing. White Kenyan Mark Wimbish found him domineering, a man who could not abide the views of others. Judy Ware, a Dunham friend, recalled meeting Obama "sometime later in Port Angeles, Washington," a rather remote place on the Olympic Peninsula where the Kenyan never shows up in the sweet and lyrical *Dreams from My Father*. Neither does he show up there in *The Other Barack* or any newspaper accounts. Scott provides no date for the encounter but Ware describes Obama (page 84) as "outgoing, friendly, and that he was flirtatious, and that made me uncomfortable. He was just a bit intimidating to me. He was too close in my personal space" and "I thought he was a little bit almost aggressive in his way of meeting and being around women."

In Scott's account, the couple meet in the fall of 1960. She is seventeen and he is twenty-four. "Though he apparently omitted to mention it initially," Scott writes, "Obama was a married man, with a wife and child in Kenya and a second child on the way."

Ann had never had a boyfriend and was a virgin, according to Kadi Warner, Ann's graduate school friend. "Some years later" Ann told Warner she was "totally enthralled" by Obama, who was brilliant, striking and exotic. According to Warner, he courted her and she was attracted to him. Said Warner, "I doubt he was the sort of man who would have carried a condom in his pocket" and "many years later" Warner said Ann married Obama because she was pregnant.

As with many a subject, the Kenyan's own views on birth control are not on record. Interestingly enough, in *Sex Rebel: Black*, Frank Marshall Davis makes clear his disdain for condoms. And he is certainly flirtatious and aggressive with women, very close in their personal space. As he said in *Livin' the Blues*, "summer sessions at the university bring thousands of co-eds intent on having a ball." And as the couple from Seattle told him, "quite a few coeds are available for special affairs."

Scott cites *Dreams from My Father* about the meeting in Russian language class and falling in love. The Kenyan's charm wins over the parents and he marries the girl, who bears him a son "to whom he bequeathed his name." He leaves for Harvard without money to take his family, then returns to Africa. The mother and child stay behind but the bond of love survives the distances.

Scott notes that Obama wrote his account when he was in his early thirties, "at a time when his mother and grandmother were alive and well, and available for consultation." But Obama (page 85), "offers little in the way of alternative version" and "It appears that parts of the account he was told were wrong."

In Scott's account, Ann gets pregnant, drops out of school and marries Obama discreetly, but there's a problem. Scott finds no record of a real wedding, a cake, a ring, a giving away of the bride, little details like that. No families were in attendance, and people back in Kansas were not informed.

In Scott's account, on 7:24 p.m. on August 4, 1961 at Kapit'olani Maternity and Gynecological Hospital in Honolulu, Ann gives birth to Barack Hussein Obama Jr. So the identity of the father and the bequeathing of his name was not the part of the account that Obama got wrong. At no point does Janny Scott, *New York Times* reporter, challenge what she calls the "family myth," a term that also appears in the sweet, lyrical *Dreams from My Father*, which also talks of a "useful fiction." Eleven months later, meanwhile, "the elder Obama was gone."

Scott then turns to the article Obama Jr. said he found along with his birth certificate and vaccination forms, while in high school. She refers to the four-paragraph June 20, 1962 *Honolulu Star-Bulletin* article, which said the Kenyan Barack Obama had departed to tour mainland universities before entering Harvard. The article does not mention the Kenyan student's American wife and son.

Scott does not cite the longer June 22, 1962 *Honolulu Advertiser* article by John Griffin. In that piece, as the author of *Dreams from My Father* noted, the Kenyan scolds the university for herding visiting students into dormitories and forcing them to attend programs designed to promote cultural understanding, which he regards a distraction from practical training. The Kenyan detects self-segregation and discrimination between the various ethnic groups, but explains that other nations can learn from Hawaii about the willingness of races to work together toward common development. But as in the earlier *Star-Bulletin* article, the Kenyan fails to mention any American wife and infant son.

The photo of Barack Obama accompanying the June 22 article does not appear in *A Singular Woman*. Neither does a photo of the birth certificate and vaccination records Obama Jr. says he found along with the article. Putting that in the book would have been an easy way to smack down those birthers once and for all, and quiet those fevered imaginations of supermarket tabloids and the Internet.

Scott's book does have photos scattered through the text, but none has a credit on the page on which the photo appears. The book has no table of contents but tucked away at the back readers find notes on the photo sources. These come from Ann's classmates, colleagues, field assistants, a driver, and professors. Some came from Ann herself and others came from "family members and friends of Ann Dunham, some of whom chose not to be credited by name." The author offers no reason why they should decline to be identified.

"Some of the images in this book," Scott concedes (page 375), "were made public during the 2008 presidential campaign by Obama for America, the campaign organization." These include the black-and-white photo on page 144 of Ann "With Barack Obama Sr. Christmas 1971," as the line below explains. The smiling Kenyan, in a suit and tie, has his left arm around Ann, with his hand resting on her shoulder. It is the only photo in the book of Ann and the Kenyan together.

Also from the Obama for America campaign is the black-and-white photograph on page 145 showing "Barack Obama Sr. and the young Barack, Christmas 1971." The Kenyan has his left arm around the young Barack, who has his arms folded over the Kenyan's hand. Two of the Kenyan's fingers protrude from below, and seem out of proportion to the size of the hand. Young Barack is looking at the camera, but the Kenyan is not. Both photos are rather blurry, particularly the background, which appears to be an airport terminal. A sign in the upper left reads "San Francisco." Readers can be the judge, but both photos have a crude, cut-and-paste look that stands in stark contrast to the photos from other sources, none of which show the Kenyan and Ann together.

The other photos from Obama for America show "Stanley and Barack" at the beach (page 94, undated) and Ann "with Lolo, Maya, and Barack, 1970." Readers get no information on any of the photo sources until the final two pages of the book. The omissions are also significant.

Recall that, in *Dreams from My Father*, the author mentions a photo of himself holding the orange basketball he says his Kenyan father gave him, and a photo of the Kenyan with the tie that the lad gave him. These photos (page 70), taken "in front of the Christmas tree" were "the only ones I have of us together." *Dreams from My Father* and *The Audacity of Hope* did not include that photo, and neither does *A Singular Woman*. So it's not a stretch that the pictures may have an existential problem.

As Scott tells it, Ann left Hawaii before Obama Sr. did. Ann's friend Maxine Box saw her in Seattle in the summer of 1961, all happy and proud of her baby but (page 87), "saying nothing about marriage." Indeed, "Her sudden motherhood startled friends" and the news of Ann's pregnancy, sudden marriage and separation was "closely held" within the Dunham and Payne families. Ralph Dunham, Ann's uncle, did not get the news of the pregnancy and marriage until after the child was born.

Ann enrolled at the University of Washington for the spring quarter of 1962 and after the semester returned to Honolulu. She supposedly divorced Obama in 1964 and on March 5, 1964, married Lolo Soetoro. Janny Scott (page 146) tracks some difficulties with that union.

"The status of Ann's marriage was ambiguous, it seems. According to Obama's account, Ann had separated from Lolo. But that was less clear to friends." According to Kadi Warner, who like Ann had secured a grant from the East-West Center, "she certainly considered herself married."

Janny Scott evidently failed to ask any of Ann's friends about the poet Frank, who gets a full 2,500 words in the sweet, lyrical *Dreams from My Father*. In *A Singular Woman* Frank gets zero words, though some accounts of the Kenyan do seem more like Frank. All told, the mysteries of fatherhood remain but Scott does shed some light on Ann's life, which shows no interest in Russian language, Kenya, the Kenyan Barack Obama, or Africa in general.

In a letter to Bill Byers (page 142), "the wheelman on the fateful Cadillac-convertible flight to the San Francisco Bay Area," Ann tells Bill she got the East-West grant, and when that's gone:

"I shall be most content to spend the rest of my life in obscure corners of the world. Probably a useless sort of life, and not very socially relevant, especially since I hate applied anthropology (neo-colonialism in bad disguise – I had a lot of bad experience with it in Asia.) I do hope to spend most of my time for the next few years in the islands since my son Barry is doing very well in school there, and I hate to take him abroad again till he graduates, which won't be for another six years."

So despite the Kenyan bequeathing his name, and Miss Hefty's grade-school proclamation that "Barack is such a beautiful name," his mother Ann still calls him Barry, and so do friends such as Kadi Warner. Ann may have considered her life useless but Janny Scott provides more detail on the American woman from Kansas than the sweet, lyrical *Dreams from My Father* does on the Kenyan. Photos show the singular woman with professional colleagues and family alike, and her legacy includes documents one can look up. In the bibliography for example, readers find:

Dunham, S. Ann, *Peasant Blacksmithing in Indonesia: Surviving and Thriving Against All Odds*, Honolulu: University of Hawaii, 1992.

Dunham, S. Ann, *Surviving Against the Odds: Village Industry in Indonesia*, Durham, NC: Duke University Press, 2009.

The bibliography includes books on Indonesia and *The Audacity of Hope* and *Dreams from My Father*, both by "Obama, Barack." So the official story, in effect, extends cover to cover, and the book appeared well in time for the 2012 elections, complete with material supplied by Obama for America, the campaign organization.

Meanwhile, Sally Jacobs 2011 book focused on the "other" Barack Obama, but readers might also find it enlightening on Ann Dunham and the parental issues.

"Obama said nothing of his new girlfriend."

For example, (page 5) in 1997, the Barack Obama of Chicago disavows any claim on the Kenyan's estate, worth about $57,000 at the time he died. When the Kenyan was studying at the University of Hawaii in the fall of 1960, Jacobs writes (page 115), he enrolled in a Russian language class taught by Ella Wiswell in Room 209 of the new Physical Science building. One of his classmates was "a slender young woman with expressive brown eyes." That description is from Jacobs, not Ella Wiswell, who was not mentioned in *Dreams from My Father*. Jacobs does not tell readers that the Russian-born University of Hawaii professor died in 2005 at the age of 96.

For her part, Ann was shy, (page 116) but "had asserted herself as an iconoclast, and independent thinker with decidedly liberal views. Like many self-respecting teenagers she abhorred the deadly conformity of the suburbs. She was an atheist who sported a campaign button for Democratic presidential candidate Adlai Stevenson and liked foreign movies and jazz. . . A dreamer like her father, she had a tendency to romanticize that enabled her to glide over human failings and foibles."

In Jacobs' account Ann is "exceptionally bright," and with a "vast vocabulary and intellect to match, she could hold her own on most any subject. And she didn't hesitate to challenge the sacred cows of her era. What was so good about democracy? What was so bad about communism? And why was capitalism so great?"

This doesn't sound much like the *Dreams from My Father* account of the "awkward, shy American girl" who fell for the brilliant African student in Russian class at the University of Hawaii. On other hand, these are not quotes from Ann Dunham and the author does not cite any of Ann's friends in this connection. Stanley Dunham, a military veteran, does not exactly bring to mind a "dreamer."

Jacobs does note that Ann's father would not let her enroll at the University of Chicago or the University of Washington "as many of her friends intended to do." Dunham and her parents headed for Honolulu a few days after commencement and (page 117), "Dunham was angry at her father, with whom she already had a prickly relationship." Ann quickly adapted to Hawaii and was soon wearing shorts and muumuus to class, and "dating an African from Kenya." In Jacobs' account "he called her Anna and their courtship was as swift as it was intense" and her primary source is *Dreams from My Father*. In this account, Ann called her new love "the African," prompting friends to ask if he had a name.

"Obama, however, said nothing of his new girlfriend to most of his friends on campus," writes Jacobs (page 118). Recall that, in *Dreams from My Father* he talked her up big time, telling friends, "I told you she was a fine girl." Soon Anna the fine American girl was pregnant but the iconoclastic challenger of sacred cows like democracy had no problem with the bourgeois institution of marriage, and that to a man already married, with children. In Jacobs' account that took place on February 2, 1961, in Wailuku, a quiet civil ceremony with neither family in attendance, no cake and no ring, the description from *Dreams from My Father*. According to friends Jacobs interviewed, Ann broadcast the news that she had married the African, was now Mrs. Barack Obama, and "we are expecting a baby in the summer." The Kenyan's response (page 121) was rather different.

"As usual he told none of his friends that he had gotten married or was expecting a baby." That is certainly significant, and nothing along those lines turned up in the cache of the Kenyan's material from the Schomburg Center for Research in Black Culture in 2013. The material dated from the crucial period of 1958 to 1964 but in none of it, including more than 20 letters, did the Kenyan Barack Obama say anything about an American wife and son.

Jacobs also found evidence in an INS memo that Ann made efforts to give up the baby for adoption, a finding of great significance.

Nothing along those lines appears in *Dreams from My Father*, and readers might wonder why presidential biographers, PBS documentarians and investigative reporters did not stumble on the adoption story long before Sally Jacobs did, say, as far back as 1995.

"It is possible," the *Boston Globe* journalist writes (page 122), "that Obama Sr., not always beholden to the truth, simply lied about the matter." She does not explore the possibility that there was no wedding, that the baby was not the Kenyan's, and that the President of the United States and his handlers "simply lied" at any point.

The author of *Dreams from My Father* is candid that much of what he told about the Kenyan Old Man was "a lie," part of the useful fiction. And the Kenyan Old Man was a prop in someone else's narrative, a character that could be altered at will or ignored when convenient. Jacobs does not explore these questions but she did find that the Salvation Army, where Dunham allegedly made efforts to give up the baby, "declined to discuss the matter, citing privacy regulations."

Robert Gibbs, White House press secretary, told Jacobs (page 123) that the president never heard that either of his parents considered putting him up for adoption and that the president had not seen the INS memo. The president himself also declined to be interviewed on the subject, still showing that stubborn desire to protect himself from scrutiny. Jacobs mentions the Certification of Live Birth "issued by the State Health Department and publicly released by Obama's presidential campaign" but *The Other Barack* does not include a photo of the document or any citations from it. Neither did *Dreams from My Father* or *The Audacity of Hope*.

In the fall of 1961, only months after the birth, Ann Dunham moved back to Seattle and enrolled at the University of Washington. As Janny Scott noted, she told her friends nothing about a marriage. Jacobs cites no sources that place the Kenyan in Port Angeles, Washington, where he appears in Scott's book. In *The Other Barack*, the Kenyan is back east, describing his family as a wife and two children in Kenya, and making no mention of Ann Dunham and Barack Obama Jr. to college admission officials. *The Other Barack* includes no photo of the Kenyan and Ann Dunham together. The book does include the photo of the

Kenyan and his son, from the Obama 2008 presidential campaign, captioned:

"The two Barack Obamas pose for a photo that was apparently taken in Honolulu in 1971. The Christmas visit was the only time the two were together after the elder Obama left his small family in Hawaii to attend Harvard University in 1962."

Jacobs does not comment on the photo's rough cut-and-paste look, but it was "apparently" taken in 1971. In *Dreams from My Father*, which Jacobs quotes uncritically, the author recalls not a single statement from that Christmas 1971 visit. The *Boston Globe* reporter does not speculate how it could all be "irretrievably lost." On the other hand, she is willing to concede that the Kenyan had a casual relationship with the truth and might have "simply lied." She does not hint that the author of *Dreams from My Father* might have "simply lied" about anything, at any time. Gramps might say that with reporters and biographers alike, this man can do no wrong and the truth counts for nothing.

Jacobs mentions Lolo Soetoro, the Indonesian student Ann Dunham married in 1965, but not their daughter Maya. She told Janny Scott that the Kenyan met her mom at the East-West center, which had not even been built at the time. Scott acknowledges that the account is "not strictly true" but still contends that "the family myth contained a kind of truth."

In the Age of the Tweet, when reporters "know nothing," as Ben Rhodes said, and journalistic frauds become celebrities, "a kind of truth" seemed to be enough for most observers. In the style of Ken Ringle, two others opted for a different approach.

"Remarkable similarities."

In 2012, as the election approached, Paul Kengor, professor of political science at Grove City College, published *The Communist: Frank Marshall Davis: The Untold Story of Barack Obama's Mentor*. This thoroughly researched 400-page work charted how Frank kept busy in Chicago with journalism and worked with a number of CPUSA front groups. Then in 1948 the Communist Party packed him off to Hawaii, where Frank wrote for the *Honolulu Record*, a publication backed by the CPUSA and the International Longshoremen's and Warehousemen's Union, headed by Harry Bridges, another Communist and Soviet agent. *The Communist* details Davis' journalism there, the same pro-Soviet boilerplate he produced in Chicago. He blasted opponents as fascists, racists, Ku Kluckers, Nazi storm troopers and so on.

Frank's primary political targets were Democrats, particularly U.S. President Harry Truman. As *The Communist* notes, Frank Marshall Davis' FBI file runs 600 pages, nearly twice as long as Kengor's book and longer than *Dreams from My Father* and *The Audacity of Hope*.

Frank Marshall Davis, Communist Party card number 47544, was a supporter of the Soviet Union. His white Party bosses were always right and the Stalinist Davis was a crusader for "the triumph of Soviet power in the United States," as his Party oath stated. This was "Frank," the man to whom the author of *Dreams from My Father* had devoted 2,500 words, but who had disappeared in the audio version and made no appearance at all in a 10,000-word *Washington Post* article on Obama in Hawaii by presidential biographer David Maraniss. Journalists and liberal biographers, professor Kengor wrote, showed "unscholarly bias" and were "dutifully doing backflips to protect Barack Obama."

As Gramps might say, they showed a stubborn desire to protect the president from scrutiny. That too requires the kind of collaboration Hugh Gregory Gallagher described in *FDR's Splendid Deception.* The FDR White House (page 93) "imposed certain rules, which were always followed." Press secretary Steve Early (page 94) said the handicap was "not a story" and the press corps played along. No newsreel ever showed FDR being lifted, carried or pushed in his chair. No cartoon showed him physically impaired, and many have him running, jumping, and performing physical tasks.

FDR, Gallagher concludes (page 210), "conspired with the public to present the image of the president as vigorous and physically fit. Now, after his death, biographers continue this conspiracy. They simply accept the image of Roosevelt as he presented it to the public." Likewise, current establishment journalists and presidential biographers simply accept uncritically the story in *Dreams from My Father,* attack those who challenge it, and ignore or downplay Frank Marshall Davis.

For his part, Paul Kengor noted (page 9) "remarkable similarities" between the columns of Frank Marshall Davis and the political actions and views of President Obama. Frank marched in May Day parades, and so did Obama as a U.S. Senator. Frank hated the British in general and Winston Churchill in particular. President Obama removed a bust of Churchill from the Oval Office and returned it to the Brits. In fairness to Frank, that action may derive in part from Churchill's comments on Islam.

"Individual Moslems may show splendid qualities," Churchill wrote, "but the influence of the religion paralyzes the social development of those who follow it. No stronger retrograde force exists in the world."

Any president who attended a "predominantly Muslim" school, and equates conversion to Islam with assertion of African heritage, would have reason to banish a bust of Churchill from his office.

Frank, meanwhile, advocated government wealth redistribution, and so does the president because, as he contends, the free market doesn't work and has never worked. Frank bashed Wall Street, and so does the president. Frank was not a believer in American exceptionalism and neither is the president, whose narrative creates a symmetry between America's past and colonialism. Frank attacked big business, bankers and big oil, and targeted corporate executives for not paying their fair share. He hated "GOP" tax cuts he said only benefitted millionaires. And Frank was fond of slogans such as "change" and "forward," without indicating what they might mean in practice. As Kengor noted, "the list goes on and on."

Readers will also find *The Communist* informative on Chicago's old Stalinist network, from which key presidential advisors David Axelrod and Valerie Jarrett emerged. As Kengor saw it (page 115), "the ghosts of Chicago's frightening political past are alive and well in Washington today." His book also detailed Communist Party influence on the Democratic Party, so no surprise that the old-line establishment media did not welcome *The Communist* with open arms and open minds.

On March 23, 2015, nearly three years after Kengor's book appeared and more than six years into Obama's presidency, *Washington Post* fact checker Michelle Hee Lee authored a piece headlined, "Frank Marshall Davis: Obama's 'Communist Mentor'"? The fact checker described Davis as a man who "wanted African Americans to have constitutional rights." Readers might note that, as a Communist loyal to the Soviet Union, Frank Marshall Davis did not believe in the U.S. Constitution, nor any bourgeois trifles such as freedom of speech, assembly, association and so forth.

According to the *Post,* Davis was only "associated with the Communist Party" and the FBI said he was a member, but the fact checker found no evidence Davis was a "hard-core Communist who spied for Soviet leaders." And she found no evidence that Davis remained a "close Communist mentor" who advised Obama "throughout his life." This lingering "assertion" got three Pinocchios, confirming a stubborn desire to protect the president from scrutiny. That should come as no surprise, given the contents.

In *The Communist*, Kengor discussed the president's olfactory "Pop" poem, which is clearly about Davis, a poet, who "makes me smell his smell, coming from me."

The author of *Dreams from My Father* never uses Pop for the Kenyan, whom he calls the Old Man. Kengor speculates (page 266) that "Pop" might be a simple term of endearment for Frank in the style of Pittsburgh Pirates slugger Willie Stargell, whom fans called "Pops" late in his career. As Gramps might say, that is quite a stretch.

Readers might recall "Sanford and Son," the popular 1970s television comedy, which would have been familiar to the president and his narrator. In this show, son Lamont always used "Pop" for his father Fred Sanford, played by Redd Foxx. In one episode, when an old friend of Fred's claims to be Lamont's real father, Lamont proclaims Fred "the only Pop I've ever known."

Curiously, in another "Sanford and Son" episode, Fred and Lamont are out to impress their sophisticated relative Osgood Wilcox, played by Roscoe Lee Browne. Fred serves wine and Wilcox says it "has a fine fruity taste." Fred responds, "Lamont, did you clean the jelly out of them glasses?" In *Dreams from My Father*, readers may recall, the jovial Frank, shares whiskey with Gramps "out of an emptied jelly jar."

Whatever the symmetry, Paul Kengor makes it clear he is not prepared to argue that Frank Marshall Davis is the president's biological father. That was the contention of Joel Gilbert's *Dreams from My Real Father* documentary, also released in 2012.

"His dad taught him to love jazz."

The film details the back story of the Stalinist left in Chicago where Davis was a big star. All the White House players are in there, including red diaper baby David Axelrod, Obama's narrator, who signs off on his every word, according to the *New York Times*. The documentary is also thorough on its central theme.

Stanley Dunham is working for the government and keeping tabs on Frank at a time when the Soviet Union has designs on Hawaii. Stan's daughter Ann, short of friends, duly shows up in Frank's photo studio and gives him the benefit of hindsight and foresight. Viewers can see the photos Frank took and the magazines in which they appeared. Viewers don't see Ann giving Frank the kind of access he described in *Sex Rebel*, but Frank didn't like condoms and, as the gypsy woman said, she soon had a boy child coming. The film gets into that whole dodge with the Kenyan student who supposedly "bequeathed" his name to the child, along with his career. In *Dreams from My Father*, the author's mother told him his career choice to be a community organizer was "all in the genes." *Dreams from My Real Father* raises questions about whose genes were in play.

In the comparison photos, as Auma might say, the president and Frank do indeed have the same mouth. Frank looks more like the president than the Kenyan, and the physical resemblance could explain the dearth of photos and documents in *Dreams from My Father* and the comparison with Nat King Cole. In reality, Gramps might say, the president looks an awful lot like Franky Davis Jr.

After comparing the photos, readers might also run some numbers. The population of Hawaii in 1961 was only 659,000, with blacks accounting for about 2 percent and whites about 30 percent, fewer in number than Japanese. With that breakdown, the odds of another white woman being a dead ringer for Ann Dunham, and another black man the spitting image of Frank Davis, are decidedly slim.

Gilbert's film contends that the president even got a nose job to throw people off the scent. The older the president gets, according to the film, the more he looks like Davis. Observers could easily conclude that the president looks as much like Frank Davis as Arnold Schwarzenegger looks like Joseph Baena, the child he fathered with his housekeeper.

Dreams from My Real Father includes some great footage of Frank his own baleful self. His voice is similar to the president's, but a heavy pall seems to hang over the old Stalinist and the words ooze out of him. The long decades of lies and shilling for white Communist dictatorships have taken their toll, but Frank soldiers on. The author of *Livin' the Blues* and *Sex Rebel: Black* reads from his poetry and explains that Hitler learned about racism from the American south. That's classic stuff from Frank.

Both Frank and the President of the United States could learn something from Hans J. Massaquoi, the actual son of a black African (Liberian) father and a white German mother. In *Destined to Witness: Growing up Black in Nazi Germany*, Massaquoi writes that he found no difference whatsoever between the Nazis and Communists, who worked together during the Stalin-Hitler Pact. Readers will find *Destined to Witness* a remarkable and authentic account, like Robert Robinson's *Black on Red*, and a stark contrast to *Dreams from My Father*.

As journalist Mark Tapson noted in a review of Gilbert's documentary, "the 'birthers' have been on a fool's errand. To understand Obama's plans for America, the question is not 'Where's the birth certificate,' but 'Who's the real father?'" This matters, Gilbert said in an interview, because "promoting a false family background to hide an agenda irreconcilable with American values is a totally unacceptable manipulation of the electorate."

The president's handlers attacked the film, and as Gilbert told this writer, "they went out of their way to condemn me, while never denying that Davis was Obama's father, nor addressing the premise of the film." But Gilbert got some confirmation in a different way. In September of 2012, he received an email from Obama's deputy campaign manager Julianna Smoot offering voters a chance to win a dinner with the president.

"You can learn a lot," Smoot wrote. "His dad taught him to love jazz. . ."

Gilbert was familiar with the president's official story line, that he was with the Kenyan only a single time in the early 1970s, and that he remembered not a single statement or exchange from the entire encounter. The biggest jazz aficionado in the president's life was Frank Marshall Davis, who writes about jazz at length in *Livin' the Blues*. In Chicago, the author of *Dreams from My Father* writes, "I imagined Frank in a baggy suit and wide lapels, standing in front of the old Regal Theatre, waiting to see Duke or Ella emerge from a gig." He also wrote in the "Pop" poem that "I see my face within Pop's black-framed glasses." Yet as far as Gilbert knew, nobody had ever directly asked the president about the man who so resembled him, physically and politically.

By this time the vaunted presidential historians had become like the hagiographers who cover the British royal family. The old-line establishment media, that faithful echo chamber, was not up to the task, but in April, 2015, Gilbert duly tracked down the Kenyan's oldest son. Malik Obama found "a great resemblance," telling Gilbert, "I think Frank Marshall Davis and Barack, they look alike. Some kind of moles I see on his face and Frank, he has those too. There's a resemblance." Malik Obama was even willing to conduct a DNA test.

"That would really prove whether we are related or not," Malik said. "Yes. I would be willing to do that. I don't know how I'd deal with it, if it really came out that he really is a fraud or a con."

Neither *Dreams from My Real Father* nor *The Communist* got much media traction in the run-up to the 2012 election. During the campaign, the incumbent president mocked Republican challenger Mitt Romney for his warnings about the dangers of Russia under Vladimir Putin. The 1980s, the president joked, "are now calling to ask for their foreign policy back," and the incumbent accused Romney of reviving outdated Cold War policies. On November 8, 2012, the incumbent defeated Romney to retain the White House.

The next year, 2013, an archivist with the Harlem-based Schomburg Center for Research in Black Culture discovered the cache of material from the Kenyan Barack Obama dating from 1958 to 1964. The letters offered insight on Barack Obama's life in America but the Kenyan never mentions his new American wife and son, not even in his scholarship applications. The President of the United States, the most powerful man in the world, showed no desire to view the material.

Readers may find this of great interest. Maybe the president was afraid of what he would not find there, that is, any reference by the Kenyan to himself, his mother, and a wedding in Hawaii. Of course, as readers may recall, he could not remember anything the Kenyan said in a visit of more than a month.

In 2014, the identity question faded and the old-line establishment media was busy covering the president's pursuit of national transformation. In 2015, when the president visited Kenya, Bill O'Reilly of Fox News explained that "his father is Kenyan." So even with media often critical of the president, the official story was accepted.

The president's penultimate year of 2015 also marked 20 years since the debut of *Dreams from My Father*. The anniversary, with the president still in office, was a publicist's dream. Ads heralding "the book that started it all," and "the dream that became presidential reality" would surely have boosted big sales, but no special anniversary edition appeared.

The president's final full year, 2016, marked the tenth anniversary of *The Audacity of Hope*. The president used that phrase in his speech to the Democratic National Convention, but announced no plans for an anniversary edition of that book. Curiously, one month after the convention, a single copy of *Sex Rebel: Black* was still available on Amazon for $275, with a single review assigning five stars, identifying Frank Marshall Davis as the author, and recommending the book "for someone who is researching black literature."

As Gramps might say, after seven years in office, the President of the United States, the most powerful man in the world, was not eager to place his official story under the spotlight of scrutiny. On the other hand, one key player could not resist the temptation to talk about it. That would be the man profiled in the *New York Times* as the president's narrator and protector, the man who sat nearest the Oval Office and signed off on the president's every word.

"Biography is foundational."

In 2015, the president's close advisor David Axelrod released *Believer: My Forty Years in Politics*, a 509-page memoir of his own from Penguin Press a division of Random House, which published *Dreams from My Father* and *The Audacity of Hope*.

"*Believer* is one of the finest political memoirs I have ever read," wrote presidential historian Doris Kearns Goodwin. "This is a thoroughly terrific book."

Other Washington insiders offered their insights.

"David Axelrod was present at the creation of President Obama's political career," wrote Clinton factotum George Stephanopoulos. That is indeed true, and here the president's narrator and protector betrays the familiar elephantine style, never using a word where a sentence will do. Consider, for example, the white White House insider describing Alan Keyes, a black American, as (page 161) "a bubbling, spewing cauldron of pompous, morally superior attacks."

Believer is also freighted with the audacity of hype. For example, the president is (page 8) "brilliant and honorable and motivated by the best intentions." The president "had major accomplishments to his credit, achievements that would help people and advance the nation." On the other hand, the massive *Believer* is about David Axelrod his own self.

In the "Roots" section, the author notes that his father, Joseph Axelrod, came to America from Eastern Europe, fleeing violence targeting Jews. Who was doing the targeting is not exactly clear. The area from which his father came is now part of Ukraine, but he did not share many memories.

In America, *Believer* explains, Joseph Axelrod listed his political party as Communist, and this became an issue when he was due for promotion in the military. So "Communist," which showed up so early in *Dreams from My Father,* appears again here, in upper case. Axelrod does not explain why his father, who like Frank came up during the Stalin Era, might have been attracted to this murderous totalitarian movement. In this account, Axelrod's father renders no criticism of Communism in the style of Arthur Koestler, Richard Wright, Louis Fischer, Sidney Hook, David Horowitz and many others.

During the 1930s, many German Jewish Communists fled to the USSR, but during the Stalin-Hitler Pact Stalin handed them over to the Gestapo. In the late 1940s and early 1950s Stalin swung the USSR back to its traditional anti-Semitism, deriding Jews as "rootless cosmopolitans." Only Stalin's death in 1953 saved Soviet Jews from the massive violence and death other minorities had suffered. David Axelrod gives no clue what his father thought about this, or about Birobidzhan, Stalin's "homeland" for the Jews in Russia's frozen far east. The author bills his father's Communist party listing as a useful act of defiance, of what he does not explain. Apparently nothing came of it.

"They figured if I had really been a member of the Communist Party," he quotes his father as saying. "I would have registered as a Republican, to throw everyone off the scent." Says the author, "dad wasn't much of a joiner, unless you count baseball teams."

From this account, the reader is to believe that his father was not a CPUSA member but the matter of throwing everyone "off the scent," is telling. Joseph pursued a doctorate in psychology and his wife Myril, David's mother, wrote for *PM*, the New York daily funded by Marshall Field, which had a "decidedly leftist bent" and where "progressive literati" thrived. One of them was novelist Howard Fast, who in 1956, after Khrushchev's revelations about Stalin, left the Communist party and wrote *The Naked God: The Writer and the Communist Party*. Fast denounced Communism as an ideology of terror and ignorance, and praised America as a land that defended the rights of the individual.

Besides his mother, the only PM writer Axelrod mentions is I.F. Stone but the believer does not name Stone's *Hidden History of the Korean War*, which charges that South Korea attacked North Korea, the official Soviet version of the conflict. Axelrod does not explain that I.F Stone was a paid Soviet propagandist who took money from the KGB.

Axelrod's mother eventually left journalism and became vice president of Young and Rubicam, one of nation's largest advertising agencies. Says the author (page 17), "I credit much of my professional success to the drive and skills I drew from her." He would use those skills in Chicago, the city of the big shoulders, as he calls it. Axelrod got a job with the *Hyde Park Herald* where he met David Canter, son of Harry Canter, another Stalinist and secretary of the Communist Party in Boston and a Communist Party candidate for governor in Massachusetts.

As Paul Kengor notes in *The Communist*, Harry took his entire family to the USSR in 1932, the year Stalin's forced famine in Ukraine claimed millions of lives, and the *New York Times'* Walter Duranty denied that any famine took place. For details on that see S.J. Taylor's *Stalin's Apologist: Walter Duranty: The New York Times's Man in Moscow*. See also volume one of *Chronicles of Wasted Time* by Malcolm Muggeridge, Moscow correspondent of the *Guardian* at the time of the famine.

Canter left the USSR in 1937, when Stalin's purges and repression still raged. Harry's son David attended the University of Chicago and wrote for the student newspaper. He also edited *Champion*, the newsletter of the Packinghouse Workers Union, which as Paul Kengor notes was the subject of activism by Frank Marshall Davis and Vernon Jarrett. The Canter family was also familiar with Frank as a writer for the *Chicago Star*, whose contributors included I.F. Stone. David Canter set up Translation World Publishers, which published Soviet propaganda.

Believer includes nothing on Harry Canter, David Canter, Vernon Jarrett, Robert Taylor, and Frank Marshall Davis, all part of the Stalinist network in the city with the big shoulders. In the early 1970s, that network was still working three shifts for the Soviet Union. Frank was legend in those circles but he's missing in action here, just as he conveniently disappeared from the audio version of *Dreams from My Father* and developed an existential problem in *The Audacity of Hope*. *Believer* has an index but it includes no entry for Frank or *Rules for*

Radicals author Saul Alinsky, another Old Left *capo* and a mentor to many left-wing candidates.

The book and its index also exclude the Kenyan foreign student Sally Jacobs profiled as *The Other Barack,* the Old Man from *Dreams from My Father* who supposedly bequeathed his name to an American child, even though a trove of his letters and documents mentions nothing about an American wife and son. Axelrod conveniently makes the African disappear, just as Stalin had Leon Trotsky airbrushed out of official photographs.

Axelrod moved on to the *Chicago Tribune* but like his mother he left journalism and began working for politicians, becoming communications director for Illinois Senator Paul Simon.

"I was surprised at how easy it had been," Axelrod wrote, "to trade in those tools for a new career, and how naturally I'd adjusted to my new role."

Readers may recall that in *The Audacity of Hope* the author draws lessons from Paul Simon, admiring his honesty, character, and sense of empathy. In the fall of 1987, the year Frank died, Simon was making a run for the White House. Axelrod lamented that Simon had worked with Reagan on a balanced budget amendment. Says the political adman (page 82), "I frankly doubted America was ready for a jug-eared bow-tied liberal as president." Note the gratuitous put-down and the negative use of "liberal."

Axelrod believes that "authenticity is an indispensible requirement for any successful candidate, but particularly for a president. Biography is foundational. More and more, I had become convinced that voters were inured to slick, highly produced media, and the antidote was this more genuine, documentary-style approach. Part of that might have been defensive, since I felt more comfortable, and proficient at, telling stories than I did creating the ads that were state-of-the-art in Washington."

The comfortable, proficient storyteller would soon have a candidate more to his liking than the jug-eared, bow-tied liberal who wanted a balanced budget. He worked with Hillary Clinton, another Saul Alinsky disciple who once worked for Stalinist attorney Robert Treuhaft, but

Hillary was not the one. As in *Dreams from My Father*, the message comes over the phone.

At one point, "I got a perfectly timed and unexpected call from an old friend that would change my life." On page 118, the believer writes:

"David, it's Barack," said the voice on the phone. "I'm thinking about what I want to do next, and was wondering if we could talk." The language is significant.

In *Dreams from My Father*, readers might recall, the Kenyan and his mother called the shots: "I would follow his example, my mother decided. I had no choice. It was all in the genes." The author also wrote: "I can see that my choices were never truly mine alone – and that is how it should be, that to assert otherwise is to chase after a sorry sort of freedom." In the believer's account, he is a mature, independent man who makes his own decisions and thinks carefully about what he wants to do next.

David Axelrod says he met Barack Obama in 1992 as a favor to a friend working on Project Vote. The first meeting was probably much earlier but 1992 is a year of significance and could well explain the reference to perfect timing.

"The narrative skill of a gifted novelist."

On February 8, 1992, Stanley Dunham passed away at the age of 73. So old Gramps, who might have thought the Kenyan student looked like Nat King Cole, was no longer around to offer insights on family history, correct any written accounts that might appear, or perhaps write one of his own. He certainly had the knowledge to do so. Stanley Dunham, the president's maternal grandfather, makes no appearance in *Believer*.

On the timing side, 1992 was the first full year after the demise of the USSR, which left Communists with lost hopes, as *Dreams from My Father* acknowledged. That same year, the University of Wisconsin Press released Frank Marshall Davis' *Livin' the Blues: Memoirs of a Black Journalist and Poet*. For David Axelrod and his eager client, the appearance of this book was a mixed bag.

The introduction, by John Edgar Tidwell of Miami University, acknowledges that Frank Marshall Davis is the author of *Sex Rebel: Black* subtitled *Memoirs of a Gash Gourmet*. Frank himself owned up to the novel and, even at a Democratic Party convention in San Francisco, a Stalinist pornographer might not get a warm welcome. But *Sex Rebel: Black* was not the only problem.

In *Livin' the Blues* Frank Marshall Davis did not posture as something he was not or downplay his Stalinism. Indeed, Frank was totally candid about being a Communist and made it clear that he joined the CPUSA after the Hitler-Stalin Pact, when many others, black and white, left for good. In these pages, Frank's white Communist bosses are always right, and white genocidal tyrant Josef Stalin, by many accounts the worst mass murderer in human history, who deployed famine as a weapon, gets no criticism whatsoever. In 1992, more information about

Soviet tyranny was coming to light from official sources. So Frank's goose-stepping Stalinism, like *Sex Rebel: Black*, was not the ticket for a warm reception, even in Democratic Party circles. Unfortunately for the believer and his client, the problems did not end there.

Livin' the Blues included photos of Frank Marshall Davis, and the selections on pages 308 and 310 show remarkable resemblance to the American calling himself Barack Obama. So no surprise that *Dreams from My Father* had no photo section, and Gramps might say the Kenyan looks like Nat King Cole, which he doesn't. The storytelling former journalist and his client, meanwhile, had a different kind of resemblance.

David Axelrod explains that Barack (page 213), "personified the kind of politics and politician I believed in. He seemed motivated by a fundamental conviction, born of his own experience that, in America, everyone who's willing to work for it should get a fair chance to succeed."

Readers might think about that. Apparently nobody in the history of the nation had ever thought of that before, and nobody in America ever had a fair chance to succeed before the advent of the believer's client.

Obama, says Axelrod, "was no dreamy reformer." Rather, he was "idealistic in his aspirations but pragmatic in pursuit of them – ready and willing to do what was necessary to advance his political and legislative goals."

This was Axelrod's guy, not some jug-eared liberal reformer like Paul Simon. The new client could "transcend race and class divides with a remarkable ability to appeal to our common values, hopes and dreams." So in the believer's view, everybody's values, hopes and dreams are the same. This was the guy who represented the future, as Axelrod told the *New York Times* in 2007. So Axelrod was down with the client, and he was comfortable and proficient at telling stories.

"I knew Barack was an exceptional writer," he writes (page 156), without explaining how he knew it. The president, after all, has that stubborn desire to protect himself from scrutiny. He never authored news stories, feature articles, reviews and such. He has not made available any senior thesis from his college days, and he produced not a single signed law review article. As Angelo Codevilla has noted, an unsigned, six-page fragment in the *Harvard Law Review* has been attributed to him but not acknowledged. Beyond that, all researchers have is a signed statement on nuclear disarmament in the *Sundial*, Columbia's student newspaper. Neither sample provides any basis for proclaiming the president "an exceptional writer."

If the client was in fact an exceptional writer, why the need to approach proficient storyteller David Axelrod? Why didn't the exceptional writer simply boot up his computer and write the account his own self? Then there would be no need for mangled sentences such as: "I cannot honestly say that the voice in this book is not mine."

Like Gramps, readers might want to ponder those questions.

The most publicized writing example was the poem about "Pop," written while the future president was at Occidental College. In this work, the poem's author wrote that Pop "makes me smell his smell, coming from me," and saw his own face "within Pop's black-framed glasses."

The believer does not cite that work as a sample of excellent writing. Even so, he says, *Dreams From My Father*, the memoir he published at the age of 33, was "a powerful and poignant work." The narrator, who according to the *New York Times* signs off on the president's every word, might have a point there. Who could forget such powerful prose as: "in spite of a stubborn desire to protect myself from scrutiny."

And like Gramps, readers might recall such poignant lines as:

"Gotta have them ribs. And pussy, too. Don't Malcolm talk about no pussy? Now you know that ain't gonna work."

And as he drives to the hoop, Ray says, "I don't need no books telling me how to be black."

This dialogue recalls Robert Townsend's 1987 film *Hollywood Shuffle,* with its Black Acting School. Axelrod the believer, the president's narrator, is like the white instructors coaching black actors in lines such as "I ain't be got no weppin." For the believer, however, it's all in the story. The exceptional writer's poignant, powerful book traces "the paths that brought together the son of a Kenyan goatherder and the daughter of small-town Kansas."

The believer does even not bother to name the Kenyan goatherder, and Barack Obama Sr., the brilliant foreign student of unsurpassed concentration, makes no appearance in the book. So the believer does not have to speculate why the Kenyan failed to mention an American wife and son in all those documents from 1958-1964. Also missing is Auma, the Kenyan relative who didn't really know Obama Sr. but certainly had a lot to say about him in *Dreams from My Father*. Neither does *Believer* cite those Janny Scott interviewed for *A Singular Woman*, or anything from Sally Jacobs' *The Other Barack*.

Obama Sr.'s son, according to the believer, "had written an entire book on his own journey on race." As the believer says, biography is foundational. And Axelrod provides some symmetry in his own story. After the news of his own father's death, the last line of the chapter reads (page 37):

"I was completely on my own."

In similar style, after the long talk with Frank before he heads off to college, the *Dreams* author "knew for the first time that I was utterly alone."

On the other hand, the believer recalls nothing of the "myth," "tales" and the prospect of the father as a "useful fiction" that readers encounter before page 25 of *Dreams from My Father*. Nor does the man the *New York Times* called Obama's narrator recall that "my father became a prop in someone else's narrative." As the believer says, authenticity is indispensible, but at this point he's not comfortable about running a fact-check. Readers will find no date for the Dave Brubeck concert in Hawaii, and no clue why young Barry could not remember a single thing the Kenyan Old Man said during an entire month. The believer duly moves on to volume two.

"What animated *The Audacity of Hope*," Axelrod explains (page 184), "were stories written with the narrative skill of a gifted novelist."

This believer is not one to hold back. Readers have heard about the incredible writer and his powerful prose. Now we have the narrative skill, not just of any novelist, but a "gifted novelist." The self-described comfortable and proficient storyteller thinks the author of *The Audacity of Hope* is *really good*.

"It occurred to me, in reading the manuscript," Axelrod writes, "that Obama approached every encounter as a participant and an observer. He processed the world around him with a writer's eye, sizing up the characters and the plot, filing them away even as he fully engaged in the scene. He has an appreciation for irony and a firm grasp on the fact that some things remain beyond our control. It's a quality that contributes to his outward calm, even amid utter chaos."

Here the president's narrator-protector remembers to pay homage to himself, like Sidney Greenstreet in *Casablanca*. And as Gramps himself might say, in this ongoing story of race and inheritance, ironies do indeed abound.

The president has one black parent and his narrator-protector has two white parents. African American Frank Marshall Davis, a man the president holds in the highest esteem, follows the ideology of white Europeans who believed in quackery like phrenology. Frank joins a Communist Party led entirely by white Americans, and his handlers are virtually all white. Frank supports an all-white Soviet totalitarian dictatorship at the nadir of its brutality. On the other hand, ironically, Frank the dogmatic Stalinist is also a swinging guy who loves analingus and anal sex.

Maybe it was true that "Malcolm don't talk about no pussy," but one can't say that about Frank. In *Sex Rebel: Black*, Frank wrote that "quite a few coeds are available for special affairs" and "for the most part it's posing nude for photographs." Likewise, in *Livin' the Blues*, thousands of coeds are intent on having a ball and "Afro-American brothers make out with all kinds of dolls." Frank dislikes condoms and has impregnated three women, all white. He would "invite trouble if I named those with whom I have enjoyed supreme pleasure." Therefore, he writes, "I have changed names and identities."

And the President of the United States does bear a rather strong resemblance to Frank, much more so than, as Gramps might have said, the Kenyan Old Man does to Nat King Cole. The president's narrator and protector, who signs off on every word, won't go near any of that.

In *Believer*, released in 2015, Axelrod was writing three years after Paul Kengor's *The Communist: Frank Marshall Davis: The Untold*

Story of Barack Obama's Mentor, and three years after Joel Gilbert's *Dreams from My Real Father* documentary. Both contained considerable material on Frank Marshall Davis and his Chicago colleagues Vernon Jarrett and Robert Taylor. Both contained material on President Obama. Both mention President Obama's close adviser David Axelrod. *The Communist* devotes attention to President Obama's close adviser Valerie Jarrett, granddaughter of Vernon Jarrett and Robert Taylor, and their connections to Frank Marshall Davis. *Dreams from My Real Father* is very thorough on Chicago's Stalinist network, and viewers get to see and hear Frank his own self. The documentary even includes footage of Weatherman Bill Ayers claiming that he wrote *Dreams from My Father*, but as Bob Dylan said, you don't need a Weatherman to know which way the wind blows.

Believer would have been the best opportunity for David Axelrod, the president's narrator and protector of his image, to refute all these nasty tabloid charges once and for all. Alas, he's not up to the task. In *The Communist*, Paul Kengor wrote (page 114) that pro-Soviet propagandist David Canter mentored David Axelrod, but Axelrod's massive work of more than 500 pages contains nothing on Kengor's book and Gilbert's documentary. Axelrod also ignores the birth controversy, even those "birthers" who focused on the location of the president's birth, not the identity of the father. The believer who is proficient and comfortable telling stories won't touch any of that, just as the president himself declined to discuss Sally Jacobs' question about his mother considering adoption.

Believer would have been the best opportunity for Obama's narrator, who sat closer to the Oval Office than anybody else, to slap down the birthers by providing the documentation they sought. The narrator won't go there, and does not reveal any of the material the president took a lot of trouble to block, his academic records, admission forms and such. But the believer does have another fire to quench.

As Axelrod explains (page 211), in *Rolling Stone* magazine Ben Wallace-Wells wrote "Destiny's Child: The Radical Roots of Barack Obama," keystoned around the Rev. Jeremiah Wright, whose sermon had been the source of *The Audacity of Hope* title. Axelrod describes

Wallace-Wells as a "hot young writer," but does not recall his lengthy *New York Times* article profiling Axelrod as "Obama's narrator."

In "Destiny's Child," Wallace-Wells wrote, "This is as openly radical a background as any significant American political figure has ever emerged from, as much Malcolm X as Martin Luther King, Jr." Actually it wasn't, and the Reverend Wright, for all his racist hatred and anti-American fury, was not the main stem in Barack Obama's "radical roots." Axelrod was doubtless relieved that the hot young writer had skipped the real back story. Frank Marshall Davis, the faithful Stalinist, was the reason the Hawaiian-born student showed up at Occidental College a pro-Soviet Marxist, and proud of it. In *Dreams from My Father*, Frank told him that equal opportunity and the American way was "all that shit," and that "black people have a reason to hate."

For Axelrod, the Rev. Wright, "however big a role he had played in Obama's past, represented a problem we would have to manage carefully in the future." The problem got worse when (page 270) "right-wing shock jock Sean Hannity" revealed some tapes of the Rev. Wright's "fiery jeremiads filled with bitterness and vitriol and anti-American slanders." This "threatened to undermine Barack's image as a positive, unifying figure. In his writings, Barack had introduced the world to Reverend Wright as the pastor, mentor and father figure who brought him to Christ," so "we were now in crisis mode."

As *Believer* explains, Obama didn't challenge anything the Rev. Wright said. Rather, Obama simply told Axelrod (page 271) he wasn't there every Sunday and that he didn't remember hearing those particular sermons. For readers who have been with him all the way, this should not be a surprise. In *Dreams from My Father*, the author can't remember a single statement from the Kenyan in a visit that lasted a full month. It was all "irretrievably lost."

The Reverend "god damn America" Wright, formerly of the Nation of Islam, was not the only problem the believer would have to manage carefully. Fox news and other conservative outlets had "run wild with a claim that Barack, as a child in Indonesia, had been educated in a madrassa, which, to many Americans, meant a radical Islamic school in which anti-Western values are routinely taught." This was (page 265) "fodder for the right-wing commentators eager to portray the Obamas as outside the American mainstream." Fortunately, with campaign adviser Bob Gibbs "and our research team on point, we were able to beat back that calumny."

The narrator shows good form here. In Indonesia the child's name was Barry Soetoro, not Barack Obama. Readers might recall that in *The Audacity of Hope*, full of "stories written with the narrative skill of a gifted novelist," the author explained that he was sent to a "predominantly Muslim school." How predominant he did not specify and in *Believer* Axelrod does not explain whether the school allowed non-Muslim students such as Jews, Christians, Buddhists, Hindus, Jehovah's Witnesses, practitioners of Santeria and perhaps secular humanists or atheists. If that predominantly Muslim school taught any pro-Western values such as freedom of speech and equal rights for women and homosexuals they are not detailed here. In other ways, however, the believer is enlightening about the president.

"Axelfraud."

In a 2008 session on MSNBC, charted on page 223, moderator Brian Williams asked what steps the candidates would take in the event of a simultaneous terror attack on major American cities. "Obama neglected to include that he would pursue the perpetrators," the candidate's narrator explains, "only after Hillary and the others jumped in to make that point did he come back to amend his answer."

So the candidate's first instinct was not to protect the nation and that continued in his presidency. In the early going he canceled missile defense for U.S. allies in Europe, a move even the *New York Times* called a "security reversal." Like those Olympic officials in 1972, he put time back on the clock for sado-Stalinist dictators Fidel and Raul Castro, who welcomed Soviet missiles back around the time the president was born. The president also seems to have trouble interpreting murderous attacks on Americans that take place on American soil.

In November of 2009, U.S. Army psychiatrist Nidal Hasan, a self-described "Soldier of Allah," yelled "*Allahu akbar!*" as he gunned down 13 unarmed American soldiers and wounded more than 30, more than twice as many casualties as the first attack on the World Trade Center. The President of the United States wondered what Hasan's motive could have been, and called the attack "workplace violence." In the president's view, the attack did not even qualify as "gun violence," one of his favorite themes.

When this mass murder went down, the president's narrator and protector David Axelrod was still sitting nearest the Oval Office and signing off on the president's every word. The index in *Believer* does not include an entry for Nidal Hasan, and the author avoids the Fort Hood massacre altogether.

Vladimir Putin makes an appearance in *Believer* but the author does not outline Putin's background in the KGB, successor to the GPU and NKVD, the organs of Stalin's terror campaigns. The believer includes nothing about Putin's role in keeping Germans subject to the control of a Stalinist police state that walled in its subjects and shot those attempting to escape. Readers won't find anything here about Putin's belief that the breakup of the Soviet Union was "the greatest geopolitical catastrophe of the century." That explains his moves in Ukraine and his opposition to missile defense in Europe suggests his hegemony plans might range over considerable distance. The Soviets claimed a right to rule wherever the czars had ruled. So might Putin want to rule everywhere the Soviets had ruled, particularly the Baltic states? As Gramps would know, Latvia, Lithuania and Estonia were the states Stalin got in his deal with Hitler, after which the two dictators invaded Poland and effectively started World War II. The president's narrator and protector of his image won't go near that, even though the former journalist is comfortable and proficient at telling stories.

In his account (page 413), Putin tells the president, "You are a highly educated man. I come from the security sector." The believer then asks the president for his assessment of Putin.

"He's smart, tough, clear about his interests and without a trace of sentimentality," the president says. As Gramps might say, that is not very strong language for a KGB veteran and expansionist autocrat.

In his narrator's account, the President of the United States uses the word "motherfucker," but not for Vladimir Putin, Kim Jong-Un, the Iranian mullahs, the rulers of the Islamic State, Osama bin Laden, any particular terrorist or criminal, or even the domestic political opponents he so despises. The target is his own speech coach, Michael Shaheen, of whom the President of the United States says (page 466), "motherfucker's never happy." Indeed, the president seems to reserve his harshest judgments for his own countrymen, and so does his narrator the believer.

Former President Jimmy Carter, at Emory University, refers to "a radical fringe of demonstrators attacking the president of the United States as an animal or reincarnation of Adolf Hitler." Said Carter, "I think people who are guilty of that kind of personal attack against Obama have been influenced to a major degree by a belief that he should not be president because he happens to be African American." Axelrod claims this made him cringe.

"If we appeared to be dismissing opposition to Obama's policies as racism," the believer says (page 379), "it would enrage all those who had honest concerns about his legislative priorities, including millions who voted for him." The believer does not detail those honest concerns about the president's legislative priorities. On the other hand, he does equate opposition to the president with racism.

Criticism of Obamacare, for example, was not due to anyone losing the health plan they liked, which happened to many. It was not due to a dysfunctional website, billions in waste, security risks, or anything like that. Nor was it the imposition of this system with no meaningful debate. As Nancy Pelosi said, you have to pass it to find out what's in it.

For the believer David Axelrod, criticism of Obamacare "was rooted in race: a deep-seated resentment of the idea of the black man with the Muslim name in the White House. The facts notwithstanding, to them, health reform was just another giveaway to poor black people at their expense." Just kind of a simple thing, but more to come.

"Some folks," says the believer, "simply refuse to accept the legitimacy of the first black president and are seriously discomforted by the growing diversity of our country."

The president follows his narrator's script with startling fidelity.

In a December 21, 2015 interview with Steve Inskeep of National Public Radio, the president said some of his critics, "may not like my policies," and may have "perfectly good reasons" for their objections. But there was more to it than that.

"If you are referring to specific strains in the Republican Party that suggest that somehow I'm different, I'm Muslim, I'm disloyal to the country, etc.," the president said, "which unfortunately is pretty far out there and gets some traction in certain pockets of the Republican Party, and that have been articulated by some of their elected officials, what I'd say there is that that's probably pretty specific to me and who I am and my background, and that in some ways I may represent change that worries them."

As Julie Hirschfield Davis of the *New York Times* spun the interview, the president was "arguing that some voters who voice fears about his presidency and doubts about where Mr. Obama's loyalties lie are reacting to the fact that he is the first black president."

That's exactly how the president's narrator David Axelrod spins it in *Believer*, in which he raised the "legitimacy" issue. As narrator-in-chief, he knows the problems of the official story, and he is now fully aware that many others know them too. But as the proficient storyteller has it, those "folks" who decline to play along have a problem with "diversity," not with falsehood. As the brilliant, honorable, well-intentioned President of the United States might say, this motherfucker's never happy unless he's dishing it out.

Actually, folks who have no problem whatsoever with a black president, including the millions who voted for him, might be seriously discomforted by the president's many lies, his statist superstitions, and the staggering debt he has bequeathed the nation. Folks who have no problem whatsoever with a black president might have a problem with his autocratic style. Remember that "higher form of power" he touted in *Dreams from My Father*. Even folks who voted for him might be troubled by the transformation of their country into a kind of Americastan, where Muslim mass murderers get special treatment.

Beyond that, and a lot more, folks who have no problem with a black president, including those who voted for him, could be discomforted that the President of the United States, the most powerful man in the world, might be something other than what he claims to be. The president himself is well aware that the story is out there, and can't be ignored.

In his July 27, 2016, speech to the Democratic National Convention, he duly invoked his Kansas grandparents and their "half-Kenyan grandson." On the other hand, he said nothing about the Kenyan student whose letters and documents from 1958-1964 contained nothing, not a single word, about an American wife and Hawaiian-born American son.

Barack 'em Up

In a scene toward the end of *Believer,* a heckler yells, "Tell the truth, Axelfraud!" The heckler might have a case, but Axelrod's confession that "I'm still a believer" does seem to be a true statement.

"Barack Obama has been a great friend and dream client," the believer says. "He is not perfect, as no one is. But he is a thoroughly admirable person, who personifies the spirit of politics and public service in which I believe. For that, and our long association, I will always be grateful."

For their part, readers can be grateful that he left all those keys near the back door, just as he did at the front.

"Without any question a work of historical fiction."

On July 25, 2016 in Philadelphia, First Lady Michelle Obama told the Democratic faithful there was no need to make America great again "because this right now is the greatest country on earth." The crowd cheered long and loud, but it wasn't all about celebration. The outgoing First Lady also laid down instruction for daughters Malia and Natasha, and by extension everybody else.

"We urge them to ignore those who question their father's citizenship or faith," the First Lady said, a clear indication that such questions remained a concern. In his own speech, the president recalled his Kansas grandparents and their "half-Kenyan grandson," a reference to the story he brokered at the Democratic convention in 2004 about his Kenyan foreign student father.

The president endorsed Hillary Clinton, and back in 2008 her handlers had been among the first to question her rival's faith and citizenship, circulating rumors that he had been born in Kenya, and showing a photo of him in traditional African garb. That was now all forgotten and the two-term president pronounced the former First Lady and Secretary of State "fit and ready to be commander-in-chief." Eager conventioneers chanted "four more years!" but the succession did not unfold according to plan.

Socialist Bernie Sanders, who spent his honeymoon in the Soviet Union, proved a favorite with younger Democrats. But as hacked emails revealed, the Party rigged the proceedings to make Hillary Clinton the candidate. She had troubles of her own, beyond the "vast right-wing conspiracy" supposedly out to get her and her husband since their reign during the 1990s.

Instead of using government-secured communication, Secretary of

State Hillary Clinton set up a private, unsecured server in her house. When this became an issue, she managed to lose some 30,000 emails and by all indications scrubbed the server so they could not be recovered. This violated a number of statutes involving classified material, and some of her handlers took the Fifth to avoid incrimination. Attorney General Loretta Lynch told FBI boss James Comey not to use the term "investigation" but instead to call it a "matter." Comey, who had a long history of helping the Clintons, duly complied and declined to recommend any criminal charges. Clinton remained the Democrats' candidate, and pundits predicted an easy win, especially given the nature of her opponent.

Real estate tycoon Donald Trump, who never served in the military, slammed John McCain because he had been captured in Vietnam. Many thought that slander would bring an end to Trump's chances but he continued to fight off Republican rivals. Trump mocked "Little Marco" Rubio, and "Lyin' Ted" Cruz, dredging up rumors that Cruz's father was involved in the assassination of John F. Kennedy. Despite that, and a lot more, Trump gained the Republican nomination and proclaimed he would defeat "crooked Hillary" and "make America great again." His own words and style would become major obstacles.

In a tape, Trump bragged how he liked to grab women "by the pussy." After that, many thought he was done but he wasn't, even though Mitt Romney, the Republicans' 2012 candidate, called him "a phony, a fraud." On election night, according to the pundits, Trump supposedly had no path to the presidency but as it turned out, he did. On November 8, 2016, voters elected Donald J. Trump the 45th President of the United States, and that marked a stark contrast to the elections of 2008 and 2012. The candidate calling himself Barack Obama gained office even though voters knew less about him than any candidate in U.S. history. On the other hand, voters knew virtually everything about Donald Trump, more than they wanted to know, but they elected him anyway.

Trump's victory stunned those "progressives" who claim to know where history is going. In this vision, if the progressive candidate loses, the election must have been stolen. The culprit of choice was Russian president Vladimir Putin, even though as Secretary of State, Hillary Clinton, like her boss in the White House, had given the Russians virtually everything they wanted. They canceled missile defense for allies in Europe, signed an intrusive deal on nuclear weapons, and did nothing as Putin grabbed the Crimea. The charge that Trump had colluded with Russia to steal the election stretched well into his presidency and sparked an official investigation. In May of 2017, as that played out, the previous president mounted a comeback of sorts.

Rising Star: The Making of Barack Obama duly showed up in bookstores. The author was David J. Garrow, who won a Pulitzer Prize for *Bearing the Cross: Martin Luther King, Jr. and the Southern Christian Leadership Conference*, which suggested the author's current subject deserved similar attention, and that size matters.

Rising Star logged in at 1460 pages, topped five pounds on the scales, and cost readers a hefty $45.00. The elephantine style, reminiscent of David Axelrod, suggested this was the definitive and official work, the culmination of everything hitherto written about the 44th president and that there was nothing left to say. Those intrepid readers who prevail to page 1084, the last page of the acknowledgments before the endnotes, find this revelation:

"Barack Obama devoted dozens of hours to reading the first ten chapters of this manuscript and his understandable remaining disagreements – some strong indeed – with multiple characterizations and interpretations contained herein do not lessen my deep thankfulness for his appreciation of the scholarly seriousness with which I have pursued this project and for what became eight full hours of always-intense 'off-the-record' conversations."

Biographers do not normally let their subject review their work in the manuscript stage and do not engage in negotiations about "characterizations and interpretations." As it happens, there are only ten chapters in *Rising Star*, so the subject essentially vetted the whole thing. The "remaining disagreements," may have been "strong indeed" but the scholarly Garrow does not bother to explain a single one. *Rising Star* comes across as a work for hire, a piece of literary reverse engineering, a trophy book intended to set a legacy in concrete. Even so, the vast text betrays more than a few choice revelations. For example, readers must prevail to page 537 before Garrow renders this judgment:

"*Dreams from My Father* was not a memoir or an autobiography; it was instead, in multitudinous ways, without any question *a work of historical fiction*. It featured many true-to-life figures and a bevy of accurately described events that indeed had occurred, but it employed the techniques and literary license of a novel, and its most important composite character was the narrator himself."

The italics are Garrow's and the author confirms what critics and even casual readers should have seen at first glance. After all, the *Dreams* author explains that stories about his Kenyan father are part of a tale, a "myth," a "useful fiction," and even "a lie."

Dreams from My Father is a *roman à clef*, and Garrow does note that "Ray" is really the president's chum Keith Kakugawa, and the author outs Saul Alinsky acolyte Gerald Kellman, the "Marty Kaufmann" of the *Dreams* account. Even so, with other mysteries the Pulitzer Prize winner keeps his distance. For example, on page 50 he explains, "how Stanley Ann Dunham's relationship with Barack Obama commenced and developed remains deeply shrouded in long unasked and now-unanswerable questions." Despite the agnosticism, the author dutifully trots out the standard answer. The Kenyan Barack Obama met Ann Dunham, a "virginal seventeen-year-old freshman" in a Russian 101 class at the University of Hawaii and by November 1960 she was pregnant.

Garrow cites Janny Scott, author of *A Singular Woman*, the definitive work on Stanley Ann Dunham, whose major source was the "sweet and lyrical" *Dreams from My Father*, the book Garrow now proclaims to be fiction "in multitudinous ways." Garrow duly recounts Judy Ware's story to Janny Scott that the Kenyan Barack Obama once showed up in Port Angeles, Washington, adding that neither Ann nor her famous son ever mentioned such a visit.

Ann supposedly told Seattle friends, none identified or quoted, that she loved her husband, but "the young couple never chose to live together at any time following the onset of Ann's pregnancy." Further, "none of the direct participants – Ann, Obama, Madelyn, and Stan

– ever offered a clear explanation that has survived in anyone's recollections a half century later." Only one person, Neil Abercrombie, a University of Hawaii graduate student, "was aware of Obama's relationship with Dunham or that he had fathered a child in Honolulu."

Likewise, Garrow uncritically cites *The Other Barack: The Bold and Reckless Life of President Obama's Father,* whose author Sally Jacobs taps the *Dreams* book as fully authoritative biography. In Garrow's account (page 55) the Kenyan tells his countryman Tom Mboya "I have enjoyed my stay here, but I will be accelerating my coming home as much as I can. You know my wife is in Nairobi there, and I would really appreciate any help you may give her." The Kenyan never said anything about "the second wife or third child" to academic sponsors Helen Roberts and Betty Moon Kirk, and that squares with a collection of the Kenyan's written materials from 1958 to 1964.

In not a single document, including more than 20 letters, did the Kenyan Barack H. Obama mention anything about his new American wife and Hawaiian-born American son. The Harlem-based Schomburg Center for Research in Black Culture houses the collection and in 2013 invited the president to examine it. The president, who claimed to be the Kenyan's son, never took up the invitation and *Rising Star* fails to mention the Kenyan's document cache. Garrow's massive account does include many members of Barack Obama's family in Kenya, with one notable exception

In 2015, filmmaker Joel Gilbert asked Malik Obama if he saw any resemblance between the president and Frank Marshall Davis. "There's a great resemblance," Malik Obama said, right down to the spots on their faces. Malik Obama even said he was willing to take a DNA test, and told Gilbert "I don't know how I'd deal with it, if it really came out that he really is a fraud or a con." In October of 2016, Malik Obama appeared on Fox News with Sean Hannity, who introduced him as the president's brother. Malik Obama told Hannity that the president showed little interest in him, and proudly proclaimed that he was voting for Donald Trump. *Rising Star* makes Malik Obama a non-person and the index (page 1438) jumps from Malia Obama to Marsat Obama. The Pulitzer Prize winner Garrow also comes up short in a more serious way.

As the 2016 Democratic convention confirmed, questions about the president's faith and citizenship remained a concern for the first family. Garrow enjoyed a strategic opportunity to lay those concerns to rest once and for all by providing authoritative documentation. The author, who is also a lawyer and law professor, is not up to the task. Readers of *Rising Star* find no birth certificates, not even the one the president released to the public. The text of more than 1,000 pages includes no marriage certificates, divorce certificates, scholarship applications, academic records, SAT scores, student loan records and so forth. Readers find none of the materials the 44th president took such trouble to have sealed, and which failed to appear in *Dreams from My Father* and *The Audacity of Hope*. In similar style, beyond the cover, *Rising Star* includes no photos of the book's subject or any major characters in his story, even the ones he is at pains to clarify.

Garrow does note that the cover of *Dreams from My Father* bore a photo of "young Barack Sr. in the lap of his mother, Habiba Akumu" but does not tell readers why publishers failed to include that information in the *Dreams* book. Even so, by pronouncing that book a fiction, Garrow helps explain why *Dreams* includes no photo section, no endnotes, no index, and above all no documentation.

As a documented matter of fact, Ann Dunham married the Indonesian Lolo Soetoro on March 15, 1965. Garrow refers to a six-year-old "Barry Obama" but Ann enrolls her son in school as Barry Soetoro. He supposedly writes an essay in Indonesian saying "Some day I want to be president."

Garrow mentions the Besuki school but does not deal with its description as "predominantly Muslim," in *The Audacity of Hope*. "Indonesia was *the* formative experience" for the rising star, according to one unnamed "smart journalist." On the other hand, Garrow's account lacks the detail of Christopher Andersen's 2009 *Barack and Michelle: Portrait of an American Marriage*. In that account, Ann registered Barry as a Muslim because his father was a Muslim, and Barry called Besuki a "Muslim school." Effendi, one of his teachers, said Barry was "definitely Muslim" and studied the Koran. Friend Zulfin Adi told Andersen Barry wore a sarong to mosque, and as Maya

Soetoro explained: "My whole family was Muslim, and most of the people I knew were Muslim."

In 2009, Indonesians erected "Little Barry," a nearly four-foot-high bronze statue of Barry Soetoro in shorts and a t-shirt, with a butterfly landing on his left hand. "The future belongs to those who believe in the power of their dreams," reads the inscription. The statue also escapes Garrow's notice, but he does not neglect other influences on Barry Soetoro.

The first word in *Rising Star* is "Frank," a reference to Frank Lumpkin, an African American married to Bea, a white woman who like her husband was a dedicated member of the Communist Party USA. The entire first chapter has nothing to do with the subject, so this may be a veiled reference to the "Frank" of the *Dreams* book. He duly shows up on page 68, and Garrow readily identifies him as Frank Marshall Davis. Since the author of *Dreams* also did so in television appearances, this is hardly a revelation.

For ten years, Garrow explains, Davis was a "dues paying member" of the Communist Party and the FBI tracked him from 1944 to 1963. Frank earned a place on the Security Index as one of the nation's "most dangerous supposed subversives" and also on DETCOM, the FBI's list of top Communists marked for "immediate detention" in event of national emergency.

Davis was also an "African American writer of significant power and great promise, a leading voice in what would be called the Chicago Black Renaissance." Unfortunately, Frank's poetry did not survive his generation because it was "too polemically political." He taught at the "Communist-allied" Abraham Lincoln School and wrote for the *Chicago Star*, an "almost openly Communist newspaper."

In *Rising Star*, Frank's wife Helen gains an inheritance and Frank hears about Hawaii from Paul Robeson and ILWU boss Harry Bridges, though Garrow does not chart Bridges career as a Communist and Soviet agent, nor Frank's duties in the Soviet cause in Hawaii. *The Communist*, Paul Kengor's thoroughly researched 2012 book on Davis, shows up in Garrow's bibliography, but Garrow does not show the "remarkable similarities" between the political views of Davis and the rising star. Likewise, Garrow ignores Joel Gilbert's 2012 *Dreams from My Real Father* documentary, which features footage of Davis and showcases the remarkable physical similarities between the Stalinist poet and the rising star.

Helen's inheritance supposedly bankrolled their Hawaii move but as Garrow notes, Davis takes a job as a salesman and the heiress Helen is an Avon lady peddling cosmetics. Frank writes *Sex Rebel: Black*, his "thoroughly erotic autobiography," as Davis explains to his friend Margaret Burroughs, an arts appointee of Chicago mayor Harold Washington and "Flo" in *Sex Rebel*. There Frank describes Flo as "quite attractive," with "unusually good legs, very sexy thighs, and a thoroughly provocative ass but almost no knockers. . . And she had another tremendous asset: an unbelievably sensuous mouth." For Frank, "Flo was my filet mignon, but I maintained my appetite for other dishes."

None of this shows up in *Rising Star* and Garrow is not at pains to provide the true identities of Gwen, whom Frank knew as "the Chick with the Cavernous Cunt," and sometimes "Old Tunnel Twat." The provocative Dot, with whom Frank enjoyed analingus and anal sex, also remains unidentified.

In *Sex Rebel*, a swinging couple from Seattle tells Frank that "quite a few coeds are available for special affairs" and "for the most part it's posing nude for photographs." Garrow does not identify anyone who might have posed for Frank, nor any of the "thousands of co-eds intent on having a ball," with "Afro-American brothers."

According to two of Davis' acquaintances, neither named, Frank and Stan Dunham were good friends. *Rising Star* admits no possibility that Dunham might have been keeping tabs on the Soviet agent Davis for the government. Dunham took classes at UC Berkeley, but Garrow portrays the World War II vet as a non-scholar who had difficulty with foreign languages. His move to Hawaii was strictly about a job opportunity with a furniture company. His daughter, whom he called "Stannie," was set on attending the University of Washington in Seattle and did not want to move to Hawaii.

In *Rising Star*, it is Stan Dunham who wanted "to learn more about black people," and that was why Gramps and his grandson visited Davis. On the first visit, Davis says "Hey, Stan. Oh, this is him?" and in this account, Stan's grandson visits Davis 10-15 times. Garrow charts the description of "Frank" from the historical fiction of *Dreams from My Father*, and Davis is young Barry's inspiration to write poetry.

In *Dreams from My Father*, Barry draws considerable inspiration from the Kenyan Barack Obama, the brilliant University of Hawaii student who "worked with unsurpassed concentration, and graduated in three years at top of his class" and became the first president of the International Students Association. With a role model like that, young Barry would be a natural to follow his father's footsteps and attend the University of Hawaii. Garrow shows no curiosity why he failed to do so. In *Rising Star*, some girl from Brentwood tells Barry about Occidental College and he opts to study there. On page 107 Frank tells him, "Keep your eyes open. Stay awake," and as Garrow explains, "with those words of paternal advice, the only African American adult eighteen-year-old Barry Obama had ever known bid him farewell for the West Coast Mainland."

Garrow does not explore what Frank's *paternal advice* might mean, exactly, but the issue comes up at Occidental when the inaugural issue of *Feast* features Barry's now-famous "Pop" poem. The subject is a poet, and as the author says, "I see my face, framed within Pop's black-framed glasses." Garrow says most readers "presumed" the poem was his grandfather, Stan Dunham, but there's a problem or two here. "Pop" recites a poem he wrote before his mother died, and Stan's mother killed herself when he was eight. Likewise, Stan Dunham was not a poet and the *Dreams* author always called him Gramps.

Everything in the poem points to Frank Marshall Davis "yet Barack would forcefully reject the Davis hypothesis," and that is enough to satisfy Garrow, who accepts without question his famous subject's claim that "this is about my grandfather." In similar style, the Pulitzer Prize winner never mounts much of a challenge to the historical fiction of *Dreams from My Father*.

Readers find the same account of the Kenyan's 1971 visit to Hawaii, the gift of the wooden figurines, and the visit to Barry's classroom at the prestigious Punahou school. Garrow says that the Kenyan took Barry to a performance of Dave Brubeck's "The Light in the Wilderness," with the Honolulu chorale and symphony and U.S. Senator Daniel Inouye serving as narrator. The only such performance this writer can find is from 1998, and in "Breaking All the Rules" Tim Ryan's January 15, 1998 *Star Bulletin* feature, Dave Brubeck makes no reference to a previous concert with the Hawaii symphony in 1971. Daniel Inouye was still in office but does not turn up in the piece. Brubeck did remember his 1951 accident near Hawaii's Halekulani Hotel in considerable detail. "I turned my neck and damn near broke it," he told Ryan. "I was paralyzed."

The Kenyan Barack Obama would be unlikely to have much knowledge of jazz, "an American musical art form," as Jazz Messengers drummer Art Blakey said, after living in Africa. For his part, Frank Marshall Davis taught a course on jazz at the "Communist-allied," Abraham Lincoln school. All told, Garrow fails to take the full measure of Davis, though Frank's remarkable physical resemblance to Barry is evident in the cover photo, taken after he was elected president of the *Harvard Law Review*. On the other hand, Garrow does betray a key insight on the Stalinist poet.

"Davis' Communist background plus his kinky exploits made him politically radioactive," Garrow says. So if rising star Barry is going into politics, which he wants to do, he can't openly tout the real Frank Marshall Davis. Garrow does not speculate why "Frank" disappeared from the *Dreams* audiobook and nowhere appears in *The Audacity of Hope*, but it does emerge that Barry shared Frank's pro-Soviet politics. At Occidental, Barry argues a "simple-minded view of Marxist theory," and he was known as a "GQ Marxist."

In conversations about his name he explains "actually my name is Barack Obama. I go by Barry so I won't have to explain my name all the time." He changed to Barack as "an assertion that I was coming of age." This is at odds with *Dreams*, where Regina, another first-name-only character, asks, "So why does everybody call you Barry?"

"Habit, I guess," Barry replies. "My father used it when he arrived in the States. I don't know whether that was his idea or somebody else's.

He probably used Barry because it was easier to pronounce. You know – helped him to fit in. Then it got passed on to me. So I could fit in."

In the 2009 *Barack and Michelle: Portrait of an American Marriage,* Christopher Andersen cites Paul Carpenter, who never heard his fellow Occidental student called Barack. It was always Barry and if someone asked what he preferred, "he didn't hesitate to say Barry." He also told teacher Anne Howells he wanted to be called "Barry." In *Rising Star* (page 124) Garrow substitutes "Barack," for his name and Howells recalls that he "spoke well in class" but "wasn't really a committed student."

Readers may recall that in *Dreams* the Kenyan supposedly "bequeathed" his name and that the African student was a "prop in someone else's narrative," and "an image I could alter on a whim or ignore when convenient," all part of the "useful fiction." Likewise, in *Rising Star*, Barry is never quite what he seems.

For one colleague he is the "whitest black guy I've ever met" and American blacks thought him "contrived and calculated." Those listening to his presentations would hiss him and want to say: "We can speak for ourselves – shut the fuck up!"

The *Dreams* narrator says "I came across the picture in *Life* magazine of the black man who had tried to peel off his skin" and claimed "the article was violent for me, an ambush attack." Garrow says it was about "chemical treatments" to make him appear white, something thousands of blacks had allegedly attempted. Trouble is, Garrow found that *Life* never published an article like that, and neither did *Ebony, Look*, or the *Saturday Evening Post*. The narrator of the *Dreams* account Garrow is willing to cut the rising star some slack. He cites psychologist David Pillemer on the importance of "a person's beliefs about what happened" because "psychic reality is as important as historical truth," given that "memory is an active, reconstructive process."

Garrow tracked down Barry's girlfriend Genevieve Cook, a Swarthmore graduate of Australian parentage who is not named in *Dreams from My Father*. On page 188, Garrow reveals the poem she wrote to him:

You masquerade, you pompous jive, you act,
but clothes don't make the man,
and I know you just coverin' a whole lot of pain and confusion
You think you got it taken care of,
But I'm tellin' you bro, you don't
You masquerade, you pompous jive, you act

Cook also thought the pompous jive was "not very imaginative sexually."

Another girlfriend absent from *Dreams* is Sheila Miyoshi Jager, a Bennington College grad who had lived in Paris and spoke French and Korean. She was also half Japanese and Garrow says that parallels her boyfriend's "half Kenyan." Further, "she and Barack were equally white, one half apiece." It might have been a southern plantation boss musing about octoroons and such.

Sheila Jager told Garrow she was "completely missing" from the *Dreams* book and "I never understood why he wrote it that way." And as she clarified, "I wonder if the unedited *Dreams* is as inaccurate as the published version."

In Garrow's account, it all began with a proposal titled "Journeys in Black and White," which the author humbly compared to eight successful books, including *Ake* by Wole Soyinka and *I Know Why the Caged Bird Sings* by Maya Angelou. Such works, the author said, "take on the narrative force of fiction." Elaine Pfefferblit at Simon and Schuster's Poseidon imprint offered $125,000 for the rights, as Garrow notes, "much higher than what a 20-year-old first-time nonfiction author normally could hope to receive." That is especially true of someone with no record of publication. Garrow does not cite any articles, reviews or features Barry might have written because there were none. Even so, he got a $40,000 advance and a due date of June 15, 1992. What he submitted, months late, turned out to be an unpublishable mess, which casts doubt on David Axelrod's claim that his progressive Chicago soulmate was an "exceptional writer," with "the narrative skill of a gifted novelist." Simon and Schuster nixed the deal and also eliminated the Poseidon imprint.

Enter Rob Fisher, a fellow Harvard law student and a Duke grad with a PhD in economics. Fisher gets the book for "critical input," and edits the manuscript. The author then heads off but not to Kenya, the land of Barack H. Obama. Instead he opts for the Indonesian island of Bali, nearly 10,000 miles from Chicago and supposedly a favorite vacation spot where he could work on the book undistracted. He could have found solitude in Key West or Palm Springs but opts for the place the unnamed "smart journalist" says was "*the* formative influence" in his life. Garrow shows no curiosity about what influences he might have contacted in Bali, where he uses Fisher's insights to "radically restructure" the book.

Fisher told Garrow he was "deeply involved with helping him sort of shape it" and "had a big influence on the final manuscript." Garrow does not reveal which passages he sort of shaped and how he shaped them, but Fisher knows the author had political ambitions and "the book was written with that in mind, no question about that." As the *Dreams* narrator said, it was a "useful fiction."

The project then comes to Peter Osnos at Times Books, the man who praised KGB-funded I.F. Stone, author of *The Hidden History of the Korean War*, as an "independent journalist." Osnos offers $40,000 for the book and makes Henry Ferris the editor. In the spring of 1994 the author takes six weeks off to finish the project and the rest is history.

Missing in action here is "Obama's narrator" David Axelrod, the closest White House advisor who signed off on his dream client's every word. In Axelrod's massive *Believer*, his old friend calls him around 1992 saying he wants to do something else, and Axelrod proclaims it perfect timing. On February 8, 1992, Stanley Dunham passed away at the age of 73. He knew the real story better than anyone, and was no longer around to correct any accounts that might appear, or write one of his own.

Axelrod left journalism because he "felt more comfortable, and proficient at, telling stories," and he specialized in presidential candidates. For a president, he wrote, "biography is foundational," and "authenticity is an indispensable requirement." Axelrod's *Believer* makes no mention of Rob Fisher, who supposedly recrafted the president's story. For all his thoroughly documented influence, *Rising Star* does not mention David Axelrod until page 820, and he comes up short on another key contributor to *Dreams from My Father*.

The rising star and his wife were chummy with former Weatherman Bill Ayers and his wife Bernadine Dohrn, and the couple's violent past as terrorist bombers disturbed them not at all. In *Barack and Michelle,* Christopher Andersen charts how Barry and Bill Ayers worked together on various projects but what most interested the Harvard alum was Ayers' "proven abilities a writer." The former Weatherman, who still regarded himself as a communist, had written scores of articles and treatises and several nonfiction books such as *To Teach*, written in a "fluid novelistic style" that the upstart hoped to emulate.

He gives Ayers taped interviews with Toot, Gramps, Ann, Maya and his Kenyan relatives, along with his manuscript and a trunk full of notes. As Andersen explains, "In the end, Ayers' contribution to Barack's *Dreams of My Father* would be significant – so much that the book's language, oddly specific references, literary devices, and themes would bear a jarring similarity to Ayers' own writings."

Garrow charts his rising star's friendship with Ayers and their collaboration on various projects but passes over the former Weatherman's contributions to *Dreams*. In similar style, he neglects David Axelrod's storytelling prowess, and passages in *Believer* that bear similarities to *Dreams*. In *Rising Star*, the major re-writer is Rob Fisher, who gets an open acknowledgement in *Dreams* for his "generous readings." On the other hand, Garrow does show how the rising star's handlers attacked anybody less than worshipful of *Dreams*.

As Gabriel Sherman of *The New Republic* told Garrow, "reporters who have covered Obama's biography" have been "challenged the most aggressively," by Obama's handlers. This recalls the narrator of *Dreams from My Father*, who confesses a "stubborn desire to protect myself from scrutiny." An unidentified reporter tells Garrow about the reason for that need:

"They're terrified of people poking around Obama's life. The whole Obama narrative is built around this narrative that Obama and David

Axelrod built, and, like all stories, it's not entirely true. So they have to be protective of the crown jewels."

Contrary to this reporter, it was entirely true that John Fitzgerald Kennedy, 35th president of the United States, was the son of Joseph P. Kennedy. The story that JFK served on PT109 during World War II was also entirely true. For his part, Garrow shows no curiosity about the multitudinous ways the "Obama narrative" might not be "entirely true." That would have been an interesting question to raise at the outset of *Rising Star*, but Garrow does not cite the skeptical reporter until page 1049. Before that, Garrow does cite those who had serious problems with the authenticity of the narrative, and with the author.

His friends Greg Orme and Mike Ramos felt many passages were "at best overstated exaggerations." Former coworkers at Business International Corporation found it "unrecognizeable" and the portrayal "fabricated." Law school friend Cassandra Butts found it "shocking to read" and said the author was "not the person we knew." Larissa MacFarquar, another law school friend, told Garrow "the contrast between the Obama of the book and the Obama visible to the world is nonetheless so extreme as to be striking." For experienced world traveler Jonathan Raban, the *Dreams* book "is less memoir than novel," the same judgment as David Garrow.

Rising Star may be intended to cement a legacy of distinction but after more than 1,000 pages the former president emerges as much less than the sum of his parts. He makes up a story about a *Life* magazine article that never existed. He's a mediocre student, often late with assignments. He comes across as a "GQ Marxist" a glib peddler of "cocky standard Alinsky bullshit," as Harold Washington adviser Hal Baron recalled him. He makes people want to say "shut the fuck up," but keeps on running his mouth. And as Genevieve Cook said, he's a pompous jive who masquerades. Those who endured his many lies, evasions and straw-man arguments for eight years will not be surprised by Garrow's monumental account.

Dreams from My Father is "without question a work of historical fiction" and the most important composite character is the author himself. On page 1078 Garrow explains that friendly reporter Richard

Wolffe, like Genevieve Cook and Sheila Jager, grasps that the rising star, "willed himself into being." An unnamed "perceptive woman" says he "is an invention of himself." For Garrow, "while the crucible of self-creation has produced an ironclad will, the vessel was hollow at its core," and as he concludes, "it is easy to forget who you once were if you have never really known who you are."

At this point, many observers are bound to have ideas of their own.

"My father was a foreign student, born and raised in a small village in Kenya," the president told the Democratic convention back in 2004. "He grew up herding goats, went to school in a tin-roof shack. His father, my grandfather, was a cook, a domestic servant to the British."

Readers of *Rising Star: The Making of Barack Obama* might not think so. The same goes for *The Audacity of Hope*, *The Other Barack*, *A Singular Woman* and of course *Dreams from My Father*, in multitudinous ways, and without any question a work of fiction. Few were on to him from the start but evidence is mounting that the president's narrative, like Blanche DuBois' tale of the oil millionaire in *A Streetcar Named Desire*, is not true "at all."

In multitudinous ways, the president's actions and policies from 2008-2016 bear remarkable similarities to something Frank Marshall Davis dreamed up. As Barry Rubin explained, the president was able "to convince Americans the exact opposite of what their experience proved," that the country had fundamentally failed and that statist, big-government, ever-higher-regulation policies "were precisely what the country needed."

In similar style, the 44th president and his handlers want skeptics to deny what their own observations might confirm. The remarkable physical similarities between Frank and the 44th president are more apparent as he has aged, but like the Kenyan Malik Obama people don't know how they would deal with it if he really is "a fraud or a con."

The greatest success of the 44th President of the United States, was greatest passing himself off as something other than what he really is. That is his legacy and how he should be remembered.

Readers of *Barack 'em Up* might also like:

"A virtuoso performance... a unique trip log of a writer who has been singularly engaged with the issues of his day," writes Peter Collier.

"*Bill of Writes* is an indispensible reminder of the long, malignant influence of political correctness," wrote Bruce Thornton, a Research Fellow at the Hoover Institution, Stanford University.

Readers might also like:

"Mr. Billingsley's book," wrote Charlton Heston, "is the best exploration I've seen of the Hollywood blacklist and the Communist Party's role in that conflict."

"Mr. Billingsley's book tells the story of the battle for the soul of Hollywood," wrote Herb Romerstein, co-author of *Stalin's Secret Agents*.

Readers might also like:

What readers say:

"A shapely read out of a massive mountain of data... dovetailing stories... a lot of sleuthing... a job you can be proud of."
— Freida Batten, first wife of murder victim Jim Batten.

"This is the third book I've read by Lloyd Billingsley. As with the others, he gives an extremely precise attention to details, exhibiting the true journalist that he is. Hard to put the book down."
— Mat Marucci, Sacramento jazz artist.

"A quick, exciting read if you're into true crime stories. Billingsley is a good writer and a terrific reporter... an author who's not afraid to overturn rocks, political and social, and reveal the slime underneath."
— Harry Cheney, Chapman University professor and film editor.

Readers might also like:

Selections from the reviews:

"A thought-provoking, fast-paced page turner, which fans of crime stories are sure to enjoy."

"Mr. Billingsley's meticulous historical research and accessible writing style makes for compulsive reading. It's the perfect book for fans of history and crime stories. One note of caution: don't start reading unless you have lots of time because you won't be able to stop until the last page."

"The story of this well-publicized murder is both riveting and disturbing, to be sure. But Billingsley also documents the legal decisions and details, in a way any motivated reader can appreciate."

For an account of this crime in the murderer's own words, readers may consult:

www.ingramcontent.com/pod-product-compliance
Lightning Source LLC
Chambersburg PA
CBHW051651040426
42446CB00009B/1081